"But now ye also put off all these; anger, wrath, malice, blasphemy, filthy communication out of your mouth."
— Colossians 3:8

"To really understand something is to be liberated from it. Dedicating oneself to a great cause, taking responsibility, and gaining self-knowledge is the essence of being human".
— Narrator - Four Horsemen 2012

Rory Wilmer

Published by Kindle Direct Publishing

Account ID: ABVGAD55O0NC5

Cover design by www.crystaldinosaur.co.uk

SOCIAL MEDIA AND THE SEVEN DEADLY SINS

By

Rory Wilmer

Rory Wilmer

Dedicated to my darling wife Jana and loving father Graham. As writers you both gave me the confidence to believe in the power of the written word and that I was able to do this. I love you.

A special thanks to Matt for believing in this project and to Bobby-the-Crystal-Dinosaur for the cover art work and chapter designs.

For my son Leon, who was conceived and born during the creation of this book. A home office child of the COVID-19 era. I love you.

Rory Wilmer

CONTENTS

Rory Wilmer

I. WHAT'S ON YOUR MIND, RORY?

Rory Wilmer

Chapter 1

Forgive me, father,
for I have sinned.

I DID NOT intend to write a book about the Bible or the Christian religion. While I have taken inspiration from The Seven Deadly Sins, I am not trying to take a theological perspective. As an atheist, I look towards all organised religions with a significant degree of scepticism. After twenty years of working in digital advertising for many global brands, I find myself having an even greater degree of suspicion for "social media" and, in particular, Facebook Inc, Twitter and Google.

I've got to a moral crossroads within myself. I have an overwhelming feeling that I should speak out. It is time to confess all that I have seen and what I, too, have been a part of—making a living and a career on the back of surveillance capitalism, data mining and the exploitation of people's addiction to social media. I've never used social media unethically. I have always considered myself a white-hat in terms of ethics and net neutrality. The boundaries of big data collection and data privacy have always been clear to me. Or at least, so I kept telling myself.

Recently I look back on my achievements and the mantlepiece full of advertising awards[1], and I think to myself, was it all worth it? Is recognition from my peers and industry enough to satisfy my soul if not my ego? Is this alone enough to keep me focused on supporting global consumerism by selling people more crap that they don't need? Probably not. A definitely maybe moment. I am taking a risk saying this. What would I do

1 Art Directors Club Europe Directory
https://www.adceurope.org/directory/rory-wilmer_9737

after so many years dedicated to social media marketing and digital strategy? Who would want to employ or hire me to consult for them after I breakdown the darker side of this medium and critique it from within? The answer took a while to materialise, but it's now apparent in my mind. Speak now or forever hold your truth. I have to be honest and write what I believe.

I no longer believe that the good outweighs the bad. That social media companies have our best intentions at heart. That they want to help us connect with our friends and families and bring our communities closer together. Their purposes focused on excess, in the form of profit - a profit created by leeching your data and selling it to the highest bidder. All, of course, with our consent. Who reads all the terms and conditions that we willingly agree to? Even if you do try to read them, how long did it take you? An hour or more? If you do read it, you will note a clause that states that the company can change these terms and conditions at any time without even informing you of why and how. In legal terms, these terms and conditions are not sound contracts. They are unfair and unjust. Yet we gladly accept them without even reading. In doing so, we allow high tech corporations to sell our innermost secrets to third parties.

Each of us has been assigned a dollar value, and the content, thoughts and creativity we share on their networks allow us to be a commodity that can be traded. But at what price? We have made a deal with the devil, sold our most private thoughts and desires in exchange for the dopamine hit of an engagement. This is how the social media engine runs on the fuel of seven deadly sins and why it is most probably harming humanity. This is why I set about writing this book to note down my observations on how social media has become a guilty sin. I'm not trying to change the world, but I would like to put on record where we are going wrong, so everyone has the opportunity to change their bad habits and take back some control of their souls. I have seen this from inside. I am guilty of using social media data to help corporations and brands sell their wares to unsuspecting consumers. It is now time for my baptism and to be cleansed of my sins.

Forgive me, father, for I have sinned.

Rory Wilmer

Chapter 2

It's dangerous to
go alone! Take this

———

I DON'T REMEMBER exactly how I got here. But here I am. Twenty something years into a career supporting global brands propagate their messages on digital channels.

In marketing terms I am GenerationX. Born into this world by Baby-boomers and proceeded by the Millennials. I was part of the latchkey generation. I suppose it was a simpler analogue time. My parents both worked full time jobs and my after-school hours left to my own devices on my beloved BMX bike. My friends and I would roam the neighbourhoods as a BMX gang, looking for wastelands and anything that would become a makeshift ramp so that we could jump and propel ourselves into the air.

We didn't have skate parks or bike parks. We had a working quarry, a train track embankment and endless fields for grazing cattle and horses. It was a great time. No mobile phones, no internet - just our bikes and our imaginations. Sure we had games consoles, but it was a balance of wanting to be outside more than we wanted to be inside, especially during the warmer part of the year. We had more than enough time to stay inside when it was raining. It was Britain, after all and rain is what we expect.

With no mobile phones if we needed to call our friends or call home we put 10 new pence into a red phone box and punched in memorised digits or we consulted the yellow pages or telephone directory books. You remember, those huge books printed on recycled paper that you always tried to rip in half just like the world's strongest men did on TV. Failing that we had figured out that you could call the operator on 100 and ask to make a reverse charge call. Something we did mischievously on many occasions making prank calls to our friends, random numbers and even our school. My first childish attempts at subverting and hacking the network. More would follow as an ever-growing love of games consoles stood alongside and in parallel to my love of being outdoors on my BMX.

My father has always been a movie lover. The first movie he took me to see in the cinema was E.T. and it left a profound memory on me. It's most probably why I loved my BMX gang so much. I would dream about riding my BMX into the sky just like Elliott and E.T. did every time I took off from one of our improvised ramps. The next movie he took me to see was Empire Strikes Back. I was never the same again. Star Wars was the greatest story we had ever seen for many kids of my generation with a vision of the future and an alternate reality where the good guys always win but the dark side's power always tempted them. This was a concept I would visit again in later life, when I was tempted to the dark side of social media and offered to use my skills for the darker side of political lobbying and political graft. Luckily my inner Luke got the better of me I got out at the right moment, changing my path so to not end up in a "Cambridge Analytica" type situation where I most probably would have ended up in prison. Or worse off, dead.

My love of technology, like most GenerationX did start at a young age. On Christmas Eve 1984 I came to the tree to open a big box which 'Santa' had left under it for me. We were living in Maryland Annapolis USA so it was custom to open your gifts on Christmas Eve. Not something we had experienced yet in our short lives, being born in the UK and following the British tradition of Christmas day being the time to open your gifts. We were excited. My sister was only a year or so old and my brother was a newborn. So I was the eldest. As I pulled off the wrapping paper one thing visually struck me right away. I knew what it was. I saw the Atari logo. It was an Atari 2600, with two controllers and a game pack. The game was Mrs Pacman. The original Pacman being so popular I guess it was sold out and my father had looked for the next best thing. I didn't mind that it was Mrs Pacman. I was just thrilled that I had my first games console. We unboxed the Atari 2600 and plugged it into the TV set. I pressed the power button and the screen lit up with the Atari logo. I was ecstatic. Suddenly I could become a rebel alliance pilot inside an X-Wing heading down the trench run to destroy the death-star. Or endlessly trying to cross roads as a skipping pixelated frog. I can still hear those bleeps and beeps in my mind as I type this. But first I had to master Mrs Pacman and not get eaten by the hungry ghosts. Power-up.

As well as having a love for being outdoors with my friends on our bikes, my second love was my gaming consoles. It shouldn't therefore be that surprising that one of my most played Atari games was called Paperboy. A game where you cycle through town on your BMX delivering newspapers to people's yards by throwing them as close to the mailbox or door as you could. I progressed from the Atari 2600 to the Sinclair Spectrum XZ and Commodore 64. Those endless hours of listening to magnetic C90 tape loading only for it to error at the last moment and you have to start the entire process again. Then something changed. Nintendo. The Nintendo NES was the moment of my life I had been waiting for as a young gamer. Game cartridges would load instantly, no more waiting for tape to load. No more failed attempts at trying to code and programme your own games based on snippets from "Your Spectrum" magazine. Now I could get the latest imported games from Japan and I could play them instantly as soon as they loaded, which felt like lightening fast speeds at the time. I was hooked on two franchises. The Legend of Zelda and Mega Man.

Of course Super Mario Brothers and Duck Hunt were some core titles and favourites, my love was in RPG and platform games of either the fantasy or sci-fi genre. Super Mario Brothers were a little, how do I say, fluffy for me. And so began a lifetime of console playing and Nintendo fanboy status. The Nintendo SNES and 64 followed and well as the GameCube. I had various versions of the Gameboy's and Gameboy colour's as well as all the Game and Watch Series handhelds. Donkey Kong and Peanuts Snoopy

Tennis being my two favourites. Being so inspired by Japanese gaming I had a NeoGeo (to the envy of many friends) and then moved onto a handheld Sega Game Gear. I'm 42 years old and I still play console games ending up with my Playstation 4 surely considering the next upgrade to the Playstation 5. I enjoy playing console games with my stepsons and wife and I will surely always be a console gamer. It is simply part of who we are as GenerationX.

My first experience of the Internet was when my father got a subscription to CompuServe for his Macintosh. My father is a journalist, author and Public Relations consultant. He was using computers from the early 80's to file press copy for newspapers and PR agencies. We had always had a IBM personal computer in the house with all the wonder and glory of floppy disks. It was during the late 80's that my father made the switch to Macintosh, as many others did. A Mac Classic proudly sat on his desk, upgrading to the Colour Classic and eventually an LCII. I'll never forget my first look at the Macintosh flying toasters screensaver. That is a visual I don't think any of us from that time will forget and from that moment on I always knew I would be a Macintosh user and not a Windows user.

My first experiences of the internet were 56k modem dial up. Those strange sounds and noises weren't so unfamiliar to me having had all the experience on the spectrum and commodore. Moreover it was a symphony of data that excited me. It reassured me. A transfer of data was loading. The protocols were working.

Once connected to the CompuServe network there wasn't really much to do. Message boards, news items and weather much like it was on the BBC Teletext channel. Teletext was the precursor to the internet. Text based pages of information transmitted by terrestrial TV signals that were searchable and navigable on television's that supported it in an ASCII text art format.

Along with the CompuServe connection came AOL. America online. And it's through AOL that I discovered IRC (Internet Relay Chat) in the form of ICQ. Instant chat messaging where we could not only send text based messages, but also share hyper links and images, in almost real time, or as long as it took for our 56k modems to download it. And this is when I started to get curious. HTML (hyper text markup language) was starting to become the main language of websites and webpages were evolving from the basic text based format that they were to become more visual and image focused and not just flashing GIFS and animated rainbow backgrounds. This intrigued me and along with Dad being upgraded to an ISDN line, suddenly the speed of my connection meant that I could start to explore the possibilities of creating publishing my own websites. Its at this point I discovered DREAMWEAVER, DIRECTOR and FLASH. Now owned by Adobe, originally it was software created by a company called Macromedia. These were visual aided tools which theoretically meant you could build a website visually without ever having to programme or code. However if you did learn to code and started to use HTML, JAVA script and CSS you could jump between both designer and coder views and quickly start to build a complex website with multiple pages and functions. FLASH allowed you to create interactive animations as well as buttons and incorporate Quicktime videos and all other sorts of multimedia elements to the page. DIRECTOR was the holy grail of multimedia software for me. Before I had tried DREAMWEAVER or FLASH I had started to create kiosk style applications using DIRECTOR.

I taught myself to write LINGO, the programming language of Macromedia (based upon basic JAVA script) and started to export Shockwave FLASH enabled websites. Through a lot of trial and error I learnt how to animate, and to build interactive websites, which were about expressing my creative thoughts and visual expressions. I had always been passionate about photography. My Father and Grandfather were keen photographers who had inspired me in the format. I was also studying Media Production at college and we had a darkroom facility where I would spend a lot of time developing and enlarging my own film and prints. With FLASH and DIRECTOR I had found a way to make my own photography interactive in a form of abstract storytelling way through the use of web based presentations.

Nobody taught me how to code. I had learnt some basics from the Commodore 64 and ZX Spectrum days but learning how to use Macromedia DIRECTOR, DREAMWEAVER and FLASH was all self taught. And I wasn't a very good coder and I'm still not. However I still gained a solid understanding of the principles and logic of what you could achieve with it. Most of all I enjoyed it. I learnt by using the internet. By reading what was becoming a huge community of forums and support websites. And that was the key to the Internet. There was a huge community. And this is the start of the journey into social media for me. The community of PHP and open source software sharing in the form of forums and websites. I started to learn some PHP which is a coding language Danish-Canadian programmer Rasmus Lerdorf in 1994. [1] Standing for 'Personal Home Page' it was becoming the language of choice for many web developers and designers due to the speed at which you could create in various serverside environments. PHP was the language the original Facebook was written in. The language of choice of Mark Zuckerberg. It was also the language of choice of millions of other programmers and webmasters. Merely for the fact of its open source support and the ability to almost make it up as you go and deploy the code on the fly and change sites instantly. As quickly as you could update a page, you could break an entire site, with one wrong syntax. PHP had its pitfalls but it also had its benefits.

In 1998 myself and few other online friends decided to create our own online forum where we could share our creativity and discuss world events. We had all been members of an

---

1 PHP https://en.wikipedia.org/wiki/PHP

American based website called dotCULT. A spin off from the FARK and STILE websites where the best writers from what was then considered the 'dark net' of censorship free forum postings would publish essay style articles. The site was minimal, clean and free of advertising banners which had started to become a pandemic of click farm proportions.

We called our forum The-Flipside. In the sense that we wanted it to be a 'flipside' from the very worst of the internet, to showcase what we felt was the very best. Community. Our community consisted of members from all walks of life and from all corners of the globe. We were young, bright eyed and looking at the beginning of social media before the term had even been invented. And that's because social media had actually been a thing long before Mark Zuckerberg arrived at university and needed to find a way to get laid. We had built a global community of people connected through a website who shared on a daily basis their thoughts, photos, videos, links to the weirdest and wonderful new websites they had discovered. We discussed geo politics, history, philosophy while always continuing to work together to make our community and website stronger and welcoming to new members.

We worked in open source PHP code and shared our hacks and developments back to the community as well as openly sharing our creativity at no cost. We didn't run adverts on our site, we self funded it and crowd sourced funds from our members - again long before the idea of kick starters had entered our modern parlance. And we were not alone. There was literally hundreds of forums and community websites popping up all over the web for all kinds of special interest niche communities just like us. In this sense when looking back with the current state of social media in mind, we were way ahead of the curve. Our forum was designed in royal blue and had a white F in a blue square. Sounds very familiar, doesn't it.

Rory Wilmer

Chapter 3

The whole world
in his hands

WE FACE TWO kinds of rulers in this social media world. The devil you know and the devil you don't. On the one side, we are at the beck and call of Californian big-tech corporations. We are conditioned to react to every notification. As the red dot appears on the bell symbol, our phones start to vibrate. We have invested and trusted all of our innermost secrets and closest friendships to them, all stored in the white fluffy concept of the cloud. All of this happens under the watchful and attentive eye of the NSA and GCHQ security services[1]. If you're doing nothing wrong, you've got nothing to hide, right? On the other side, totalitarian regimes have total control of the networks. Only sanctioned networks can be accessed. Moderated content can be viewed; anything against the ideology of the ruling party is censored. Nothing unwanted gets through the 'great firewall'. What both sides have in common is that we all live under a system called Surveillance Capitalism. The data exhaust we leave behind is worth more than gold, and the people who can mine this resource are the proprietors of great wealth and great power.

I don't want this book to be about numbers and data. That can often be misleading and act as a flash grenade of distraction. However, there are some numbers and data points that we just can't ignore. In the year 2020, there are 3.80 billion active social media users. 50% of the global population has at least one social media profile. 67% of the worldwide population (5.19)

---

1 Why we're taking the UK government to court over mass spying https://www.amnesty.org.uk/why-taking-government-court-mass-spying-gchq-nsa-tempora-prism-edward-snowden

billion people have a mobile phone capable of connecting to the Internet. Mobile phones are the preferred connection of choice, with 98% of users connecting to Facebook by their mobile device. Social media continues to grow year on year. From January 2019 to January 2020, active users increased by 9.2%, adding another 321 million user profiles to the networks. Facebook dominates the landscape when we look at the most used social platforms by a monthly active user statistic. 2.4 billion people are actively using Facebook each month. Source: Hootsuite Digital 2020: Global Digital Overview[2].

It's Mark Zuckerberg's goal to ensure that everyone on planet Earth has a Facebook profile[3]. With 50% of the world's population owning at least one social media profile, his progress seems unstoppable. Yet by 2007, things were starting to plateau for Facebook with around 90 million people signed up. A long way off Mark's goal. So what happened to get the site from 90 million registered profiles to having 2.4 billion active monthly users? What happened was the Growth Team and a tool they developed called "People You May Know".

The way it actually worked has never been openly admitted to by Facebook but what we can gather from the available evidence is as follows. If someone hadn't already created a profile by themselves, Facebook would create a 'dark' profile for you. Just in case you wanted to join, it would be ready and waiting

2 Hootsuite Digital 2020: Global Digital Overview. https://www.hootsuite.com/resources/digital-2020
3 Zuckerberg Wants Everybody on Facebook by 2020 https://gizmodo.com/zuckerberg-wants-everyone-to-be-on-facebook-by-2020-1733199414

for you. This way, when people uploaded photos of their friends and family who didn't have a Facebook account, they could still be tagged. An email would be sent to this person informing them that they had been tagged in a photo. And who wouldn't want to go and see what kind of picture had been uploaded of them, just to make sure it wasn't inappropriate or totally cringe-worthy. This directly connects into your cognitive biases. A variation of the cocktail party effect. The cocktail party effect is our ability to filter out noise and focus on one thing. If someone says your name on the other-side of a room in a crowded cocktail bar you will most likely be able to hear it. Being informed someone has uploaded and shared a picture of you, without showing the picture first, grabs your attention and requires you to see exactly what the picture is. We all like to control our image and how we are perceived by others so when someone else makes and shares a photograph of you, you wan't to be sure its not a gurner. According to Daniel Kahneman, attention is generally determined by arousal; a general state of physiological activity [4]. What better way to arouse someones attention by informing them there is a picture of themself live on a network that they first must signup to see and approve.

The 'People You May Know' function also allowed users to send invites and connect to profiles of people based on their social connections and, moreover, their email contacts. It was a friend of friends situation. You would see recommendations

4 Kahneman, D. (1973). Attention and effort. Englewood Cliffs, NJ: Prentice-Hall.

on the sidebar suggesting new people to connect to. While this idea would surely lead to a growth in user profiles, it would also have the knock-on effect of diluting your connections to a lower degree of quality. Thus decreasing your newsfeed's quality by having more links to people you had less in common with. Yet, the quality of your experience wasn't of concern at this point in time. Network growth was the main focus to realise the goal of connecting the entire world on Facebook. How did Facebook get hold of all these email addresses? Through crawling and trawling data mining techniques and the sharing of email contact lists from users who had signed up not reading the terms and conditions of the service and willingly handed over millions of email contacts to Facebook in doing so. Mark Zuckerberg's first attempts at social network platforms, 'FaceMash', used these very data mining, crawling, and scraping techniques to grab his fellow students' images and data. Zuckerberg was already morally skewed in his approach towards leeching personal data. He would have no issues with what the Growth Team wanted to do to meet his demands. "People You May Know proved to be one of Growth Circle's most effective tools, and also one of its most controversial ones."

People You May Know was the brainchild of Chamath Palihapitiya and the growth team, or 'Growth Circle' as he called it, that he created at Facebook. The feature wasn't a Facebook invention; it had already been used on LinkedIn, but much like most things at Facebook, tools are copied and repackaged as their own. The scale at which People You May Know was deployed on Facebook was far greater than on Linkedin. The unethical consequences it created was on a much grander scale.

"A sex worker found Facebook recommending her clients, who did not know her true identity. A sperm donor got a suggestion for the biological child he never met."

Facebook had never publicly acknowledged or explained how the People You May Know feature worked. In Steven Levy's book Facebook, the inside story, it goes into great details surrounding the Growth Circle's work [5]. Kashmir Hill of Gizmodo was one of the many journalists who studied the feature, searching for clues to the mystery of what is possibly the most significant growth hack of modern times [6].

"Hill unearthed the story of the woman who got a Facebook suggestion that she friend the mistress of her long-absent father. And Hill herself was stunned to find that someone on her own suggestions turned out to be a great-aunt she'd never met. Facebook did not provide her with the information she requested on how it made this connection. Later, Hill would also write about the psychiatrist who discovered that Facebook was suggesting that her patients make friend connections with each other — even though the psychiatrist did not friend her

5 The Untold History of Facebook's Most Controversial Growth Tool https://marker.medium.com/the-untold-history-of-facebooks-most-controversial-growth-tool-2ea3bfeaaa66

6 'People You May Know:' A Controversial Facebook Feature's 10-Year History https://gizmodo.com/people-you-may-know-a-controversial-facebook-features-1827981959

patients on Facebook."

Facebook has never explained it or owned up to the unethical consequences of its growth hacking tactics. However, in later years, Palihapitiya would indicate that dark profiles did, in fact, exist and that they were exploited by the Growth Circle team. So if it had ever been your intention never to have a Facebook profile, you had one without even ever knowing or consenting to it.

Social media has two distinctive sides to it. The silicon valley tech giant version and the eastern great firewalled side of Zhonghua Renmin Gongheguo (also known as the People's Republic of China). In-between the two great ideological oceans lie Russia, caught between allowing its citizens to use 'Californian social media', where its citizens' data is transferred to Langley, Virginia, for deeper analysis. On the flipside, it also supports providing homegrown alternatives in the form of VKontakte (VK is basically a copy and reverse-engineered version of Facebook), OK.RU and Moi Mir (my world, a photo, video and music network which is part of Russian email service mail.ru) to name just a few. And by now, we are all very much aware of the "Russian Troll Farms" out of Saint Petersburg who actively uses Twitter, YouTube and the comments sections on newspapers to propagate pro-Kremlin narratives and sow discord and amplify polarisation against any of its perceived enemies as a form of leverage. We are all very aware of who helped "45" get elected in

2016, and so were the FBI and CIA!

Russian authorities prefer their citizens to use Russian language web services. Hence, they have complete control over the data and the surveillance of their users. The data stays in Russia. And data that remains in Russia works for Russia. While there has been recent talk of censoring Russian access to Facebook, Twitter, YouTube and Instagram, it would be challenging for the authorities to shut them down like in China. As Russian usage of social media has very high penetration. A younger population would surely uprise at the thought of the beloved Instagram and YouTube being taken away from them. As of writing this book, we have seen the most significant protests occur in Russian modern history in support of Alexi Navalny. Navalny, who has been jailed for refusing to die at the hands of his FSB assassins from Novichok nerve agent poisoning, has created such outrage in Russia that people have taken to the streets like never before. Inspired by their brothers and sisters in Belarus who are 200+ days into their ongoing battle to reclaim democracy from the lunatic tyrant and Kremlin stooge Alexander Lukashenko. Russians are fed up with 20 years of dictatorial rule by the mafia firm of oligarchs and state security services headed by Vladimir Vladimirovich Putin. Too much wealth has been allegedly stolen from state-owned companies. Simultaneously, many families close to the Russian leadership got super-rich; the rest of the population suffers and lives in almost abject poverty.

A nation rich in resources with enough wealth that every citizen could feel like a Norwegian on payday. Russian people have again been subjected to the most humiliating violation of their fundamental human rights and opportunity to prosper. Well, in steps a teenage girl, her mobile phone and her TikTok account. One act alone encouraged people to protest and pretend to be America tourists so the police wouldn't arrest them enough to inspire hundreds of thousands of protesters to the streets. Navalny and his team have run a very savvy digital campaign with a very tight strategy. His use of YouTube and social media is a textbook on how to get your presentation and tone of voice right for the internet and social media generations. Navalny's use of MEMEs, jump cuts and editing style. His narrative and overall presentation of complex investigations into the alleged corruption and crimes of Putin and his associates are delivered perfectly for social media format. The latest video about Putin's Palace, gaining over 108 million views in less than two weeks. As Navalny now sits in prison awaiting his longer-term fate, Russian has started it's journey into the post-Putin future. A future where a younger, internet savvy and socially connected generation of protestors armed with nothing more than mobile phones will try to change the course from tyranny and back to a form of democracy.

China hasn't experienced social media uprisings yet in the same way, Russia and most of the Arab world have experienced in the past decade. China has managed to penetrate into Western social media and popular culture through the TikTok application. A variant of Snapchat and Vine apps where users can create short video clips synchronised to music songs or sound effects. The application allows for some video editing with a range of filters that can be applied to create visual effects and animation styles. What made TikTok stand out from Snapchat, which had been leading as the youth application of choice for a long time, was the aspect of TikTok challenges. A way to challenge the community to participate in a MEME or a video using the same song and creating your own version and variation of the trend/challenge. This one aspect alone, I feel, is what drives the success and appeal of TikTok. It is a global karaoke video booth.

TikTok audiences are far more active and creative than Facebook. This is because of a shift in the age demographics between the networks. The appeal and popularity of Facebook as a site for creating content has shifted to a place to consume mainstream content such as news and magazine-style content. Facebook is the world's most extensive classified ads page and just an endless stream of clickbait. Whereas TikTok is a steady stream of original content that is easy to consume and not calling the users to continually click out of and leave the site or experience. Facebook is literally a dying network. According to an Oxford University study, there could be more deceased users than living ones on Facebook by around 2070—perhaps as many as 5 billion by 2100. It is a site destined to become the worlds virtual cemetery. 'Deadbook'.

In November 2020, I wrote a blog post on LinkedIn and shared it on my own website. It discussed how I felt that creative and advertising agencies were becoming less relevant when it came to digital and social media experiences. I used the example of TikTok user Nathan Apodaca who created one of the most viewed TikToks to date whilst sipping Ocean Spray cranberry juice rolling down the highway on his skateboard. This is a prime example of who the audiences now create the creative trends as agencies can try to chase and recreate them.

DUDE, HOLD MY CRANBERRY JUICE.
OR HOW CREATIVE AGENCIES ARE BECOMING IRRELEVANT.

As consumer behaviour shifted towards a prolonged lockdown, global brands and their creative agencies felt the pinch. Brands have been struggling to come to terms with what this means, and even more so have their creative agencies. Agencies and marketers have drifted between mundane and self-absorbed when it comes to creative output during this plague season. There's been plenty of morose black and white videos telling us how much brands care about us and how they have got our backs. To wash our hands and keep our distance. But who believes this bullshit anymore? Not many people if the video view play counts are anything to go by. We don't need another PSA from brands. We have our technocratic governments to do that. What we expected from brands and their agencies was to be entertained. To be given some hope. To distract and reflect on what really matters. And they failed.

Then as if by magic, in rolls Nathan Apodaca, 37, of Idaho Falls. He recorded a laid-back video on TikTok while riding a skateboard downhill and drinking Cran-Raspberry juice. The Internet went wild and streamed Fleetwood Mac with Ocean Spray selling out of Cranberry juice in less than a week. Nathan Apodaca's story is something we can all relate to. His truck was tired, having already clocked up some 320,000 miles. On his way to work one morning, the vehicle broke down on the highway in Idaho Falls, about 2 miles from the potato warehouse where Apodaca has worked for nearly two decades. He always carried his skateboard in the truck; it wasn't the first time his vehicle had broken down for such a circumstance. Grabbing his board and his bottle of Ocean Spray, he hit the tarmac and started to roll the last few miles to work to ensure he wouldn't be late clocking on. Without seemingly a care in the world, he pulls out his mobile phone and starts to film his ride on TikTok while lip-syncing to the timeless Fleetwood Mac song Dreams. Little did he know when he hit the share button that this clip would become the most viewed viral video of the month, if not the year. The impact of this video was not just a viral one; it had a real economic impact.

And it paid dividends to Nathan as his clip seemed to capture the moment so perfectly – a moment that creative agencies and brands fail to grasp even considering their vast budgets and creative talents.

A MEME has more power than a CAMPAIGN. When I heard 'Dreams,' that's when I figured, 'OK, this is it,'" said Apodaca, a 37-year-old father of two. After the video took off, that 1977 hit single, "Dreams" by Fleetwood Mac, catapulted back on the charts, tripling in sales. The band also reported its best week ever on streaming.

In its first hour on TikTok, the video gathered some 100,000 views. It now has more than 71 million. It has been crowned with MEME status. According to figures from TikTok, 250,000+ tribute videos have been made, inspired by Apodaca, totalling almost a billion views. And then something magical happened, as reported by NPR. Mick Fleetwood, the legendary band's drummer, was so touched that he recorded his version on a skateboard, juice in hand. "It was spontaneous. It was heartfelt. It was fun, and God knows we need some of that right now," Fleetwood told NPR from his home in Maui, Hawaii. "To some extent, it was a lovely accident," Fleetwood said. "It could have been any song, but it was ours. For us bunch in Fleetwood Mac, the inspiring thing was that it was just so off the wall. Did we expect it? No. Are we happy and delighted? Absolutely."

What was the magic formula for the success of this

video? Well, it is quite simple. There is currently so much chaos and uncertainty in the world. This clip managed to capture a moment of calm, of pure simplistic joy. Life goes on, no matter what is happening. While brands and agencies are scratching the heads and their balls, wondering what to do next, the Internet and its audience are getting on with their lives as best they can. And it's important to remember this. I have never worked on any campaign that could generate more than a couple of millions of views over two weeks and which had significant media spend support to do it. Creative directors and Brand managers are trying too hard to be too clever and too cinematic. They miss the true essence of what digital is. It is not TV, and it is not cinema. While they chase outdated trends and try to make content to fluff out their portfolios or to win creative awards, they often miss the wave of what digital offers. The moment. The spontaneous and glorious moment of enjoying the flipside.

Ocean Spray recognised this. After seeing such a spike in their sales as a direct result of one TikTok video, they did the right thing and donated a brand new truck to Nathan. Much respect to that marketing team understands that one man has done more for their brand this year than any creative agency has in the past decade.

"Businesses are prioritising survival for now, but in the future will have to find new ways of brand-building. The change in people's media and consumption habits will force a rethink of how best to do so." Brian Wieser.

THE UPSETTER

MY BLOG POST caused a bit of stir within the industry. Creative directors from some of the worlds leading agencies weighed in, upset with what I was suggesting. What was interesting to see was that former creative directors of big agencies who had left the agency world were in support of what I was saying. Whereas creatives, who were still entrenched deep within the agency structure, were coming across as upset and quite salty in their replies to me on LinkedIn. They can't comprehend that the audience is often far more creative than the professionals. And they have all the tools at their fingertips and the power of social media publishing to create content that can spread across the world like wildfire with added gasoline. Something agencies struggle to do without massive investment in media spend to push their content to audiences rather than to have the audiences seek out the content natively and organically. Social media has firmly placed creativity in the hands of the users and for the first time in history way from the creative professionals in advertising who for so long felt relatively safe and smug in their agency bubbles driven by award ceremony focused driven egos. TikTok is yet another tool in every increasing kit that leads to the democratisation of creativity and content.

TENCENT

AS WELL AS generating access to TikTok for users across the globe, China has its own closed ecosystem of social media within the Tencent family. Tencent was founded in 1998. Incorporated not in China but in the Cayman Islands with initial funding from venture capitalists. Their first product was a messenger application called OICQ. They later changed to be called QQ due to a legal threat from AOL, the owner of ICQ messenger. In the first three years of the company's existence, it didn't make any money. In 2001 a South African media company called Naspers bought up 46.5% of Tencent's shares. In 2004 Tencent Holding Ltd went on to be listed on the Hong Kong Stock Exchange and, within four years in 2008, was added to the Hang Seng Index. Income to Tencent was generated by premium users of QQ who paid a subscription. Subscribers would receive extra features and bonuses in comparison to the free members. In parallel to the subscription service, Tencent was also starting to license games developed in South Korea, such as Crossfire and Dungeon Fighter Online, selling them as virtual goods.

You had probably never heard of QQ. Until you realise the name, it goes by today. WeChat. Tencent and its family of apps are much more than Facebook and something so impressive to Mark Zuckerberg. For example, with WeChat, you can make direct payments from your phone using WeChatPay. It is literally accepted by everyone in China. From major corporations to market traders. It has become an everyday part of life, replacing minted coins and paper notes as the currency transaction of choice. Chinas contactless payment advancement works because of mobile phones and mobile networks' penetration across the population and the ease in which you can make a payment. This is a product and function of WeChat that Californian social media giants can only dream of. Mark Zuckerberg's concept for his Facebook crypto currency LIBRA (now called Diem) is already way behind schedule. "The Diem payment system is built on blockchain technology to enable the open, instant, and low-cost movement of money. People will be able to send, receive, and spend their money, enabling universal access to financial services." So says the mission statement on the Diem website.

Facebook aim to be the first western social media company offering a blockchain cryptocurrency that avoids volatility through the backing of FIAT currencies and US treasury securities. In other words, existing currencies such as Dollars, Pounds sterling and Euros. It is still yet to be seen if Facebook can jump into finance and the cryptocurrency market place to use the power of the network and messenger app to become the digital wallet of choice for Earth's population.

Moving back to Tencent, it is now more than just WeChat and QQ instant messaging. The Tencent family offers a complete range of social media services, applications and uses, financial investing, banking, film and entrainment, gaming, news, and services. Tencent dominates all aspects of digital and social media use in China and within the Chinese population globally. It describes its self on its corporate website as "connecting people, services and devices, connecting enterprises and future technologies, fostering win-win ecosystems for everyone". A win-win ecosystem for a political regime which, as early as 2009, started rolling out a 'social credit system' a unified system for recording individuals, businesses "trustworthiness". What you say and do on social media and your financial history all contribute to your overall social score. A plotline from Charlie Brookers Black Mirror Nose Dive episode or right out of George Orwell's 1984 book.

This book was supposed to be a fable, not a guidebook on how to implement totalitarian control through media use. Yet here we are in a world where both sides of the ideological divides, the so-called "free west" and the "not so free east", both employ the mechanics and tactics of surveillance capitalism to monitor and exhort control over users behaviour.

INSURRECTION OF THE MIND

AS WE ENDED the year 2020, something monumental happened as a result of social media gone wild. The 45th President of the United States of America was banned from Facebook, Twitter,

Instagram, YouTube, as well as all the other major social media websites, messenger apps, and e-commerce platforms for inciting an insurrection which leads to the storming of the Capitol in Washington DC after which thousands of armed protestors tried to stop the counting of the electoral college votes and in-turn trying to enact a Coup d'état.

Was social media really the driving force behind this sequence of events? If so, how did we get to this point where an angry mob of conspiracy theorists can be inspired into acts of violence by the Tweets of the commander-in-chief of the most powerful nation on Earth. How could a Coup d'état be organised through Facebook groups with RVSP and invites through Facebook events not unnoticed, monitored and stopped? Moreover, how could the platform of Facebook amplify an insurrection and support it as being the primary source and publisher of the very 'Fake News' and mistruths and non-facts that conspiracy theorists base their ideology on?

What will be the long term consequence of banning "45"? De-platforming has become all the rage lately, with many profiles and celebrities finding themselves victim to the tech companies' ever shape-shifting policies, Twitter, Google, and Facebook. Sites that initially advocated and stuck up for the rights and principles of free speech are now very much the ones who deny it. Well, OK, why not. After-all private companies have no statutory rights to uphold any free speech principles and freedom of expression.

They are corporations whose free to use policies that we all click agree to, without having read the pages of confusing and gibberish legal-speak terms and conditions, which all ultimately are meaningless as all have a clause that they can be changed at any moment without your consent, are the biggest contractual frauds in the history of contracts. Yet still, we click 'agree'. We submit our digital permission to allow these corporations access to our deepest and darkest thoughts, fears, loves, wants, desires and creativity in exchange to be in contact with our friends and family and to find a wider audience out there in the general public and vastness of cyberspace and the world wide web. To own and manage our profiles and identities to manicure and manage our online personas and to build our network of personal and professional connections. In many ways, this contract, this agreement to the terms of conditions and surrendering personal data in exchange for free to use the software, is nothing short of dealing with the devil. We exchange our soul for diabolic favours.

We agree that the corporation can monitor everything we do online. We agree that they can see our personal messages and collect endless amounts of data that we leave behind in a cloud of exhaust as we spend hours a day and hundreds of hours per week immersed inside their social graphs. We agree that they can sell our personal data to third-parties. That they can profile us to sell us personalised and targeted products. We agree that they can send us notifications when we are sleeping. We agree that they can track our movements and monitor what locations we were visiting and who we were with. We agree to all of these highly personal things. We allow the devil to send it's minions to track us. To peer deeply into our soul and to understand us better than we know ourselves. And for what? Dopamine hit— the simple yet addictive experience of the release of dopamine.

When you see any kind of engagement on or around your social media posts or inbox, your brain releases dopamine. A like, share or comment. A new message in your chat inbox. A recent post from your favourite band. It doesn't matter what the notification is. That little bell icon with the red dot on it tells your brain one thing. Release more dopamine. We have been trained like Pavlov's dog to react on demand to the notificaion bell.

Rory Wilmer

Chapter 4

Engage or die

WE HAVE A saying in social media marketing. Engage or die. Our key performance indicators are always dominated by the amounts and types of engagement and interaction we can wean from the unsuspecting targets of our content. Something I learnt very early on was the notion that angry people click more. How you could incite people to feel negative emotions in order to lead them somewhere or to get them to engage and share their thoughts and feelings without them even realising they had been manipulated into joining a conversation. More often than not, this conversation would become an argument. The angrier people would become, the more they would respond. This led me to start thinking about the main themes and types of content that people 'share' on their own social media and what were the ultimate triggers for engagements.

We tend to project an image of ourselves on our social feeds, of the person we want people to believe we are and not really show the person we truly are. Let's face it, mostly because our lives are mediocre at the best of times and often quite repetitive and unfulfilling. When we stare into the black mirror of our phones, we are able to create the image of ourselves that we want to see. Yet this social mask betrays us, for the data exhausts we leave behind show our true selves to the ones who collect the data. Allowing them to see deep into our psyche and to know and understand us better than we understand ourselves.

This is when I had my divine inspiration. What were the

things that gained the most engagements when it came to social media. The more looked into it the more I started to see a pattern and how much this pattern started to look like a list of the capital vices.

Thankfully I am not alone. It's dangerous to go alone. In recent years many other voices have started to speak out about the perils of social media addiction. They range from industry insiders to psychologists and investigative journalists. In 2020 Netflix produced a documentary titled The Social Dilemma [1]. The film presented the opinions of many ex-employees of companies such as Facebook, Twitter, Pinterest and Google. These voices were not just disgruntled staff with an axe to grind. They were people in very senior positions within these companies. All of who now openly talk about the path in which social media has taken and warning of the terrible consequences if action is not taken. What was most remarkable about the film was how many of the people who built social media as we know it today, refuse to let their own children use the networks while heavily restricting their own personal use of it. This is because the fundamental design principles of social media ensure that they nurture addictive traits and behaviours. How they are primed to facilitate the distribution of conspiracy theories and that they have had a profound and unwelcome impact on mental health, to the point of being a leading cause of suicide for teenagers.

---

1 Hate Social Media? You'll Love This Documentary
https://www.wired.com/story/social-dilemma-netflix-documentary/

Social media corporations prolific and exponential financial gains are generated through the application of surveillance capitalism and data mining. To learn more about the this subject I highly recommend reading The Age of Surveillance Capitalism by Shoshana Zuboff. This book is an in-depth history and analysis of surveillance capitalism and its application and why and how it so dangerous for our civilisation in the long term.

Social media algorithms are sexist. These algorithms are racist. The algorithms are biased. Algorithms are not interested or concerned with the truth or with facts. This is not how they have been designed to function on social media. Not because of the nature of the people who code them. By the very nature of the way in which they have been deployed. Journeyman films conducted an investigation which uncovered that recruitment algorithms where found to perpetuate sexist hiring processes. Code which is written by white men, tends to be biased in favour of, white men. Your newsfeed is designed to keep you on the platform for as long as possible and with many returning sessions within a day. The sites and news feeds are designed to prolong usage, to create an addictive state of mind, to keep you returning and staying for longer each time at multiple points throughout each waking moment of your day (and night).

Who better to explain this addictive state of mind than Sean Parker, the founding president of Facebook. Speaking at a Philadelphia conference in 2017 he said: "The thought process that went into building these applications, Facebook being the first of them ... was all about: 'How do we consume as much of your time and conscious attention as possible?' That means that we need to sort of give you a little dopamine hit every once in a while, because someone liked or commented on a photo or a post or whatever. And that's going to get you to contribute more content and that's going to get you ... more likes and comments ... It's a social-validation feedback loop ... exactly the kind of thing that a hacker like myself would come up with, because you're exploiting a vulnerability in human psychology. The inventors, creators – me, Mark [Zuckerberg], Kevin Systrom on Instagram, all of these people – understood this consciously. And we did it anyway [2]."

So why do social media sites and especially Facebook and Instagram want to take as much time of your attention each day? Time is literally money. Every second of everyday the algorithms manage an advertising auction, willing to serve an advert or sponsored content to a user to the highest bidder. These auctions happen instantaneously and within milliseconds. The more adverts which can be served, the more revenue the company creates from the ever increasing digital budgets of advertising agencies and their clients. It is not hard to see where the majority of this money has been spent over the past decade of digital advertising. A quick look at the annual revenue

2 'Never get high on your own supply' – why social media bosses don't use social media.
https://www.theguardian.com/media/2018/jan/23/neverget-high-on-your-own-supply-why-so-cial-mediabosses-dont-use-social-media

of Facebook will tell a story of the power of data mining in the surveillance capitalist world.

In 2020, Facebook's revenue amounted to roughly $86 billion US dollars, up from $70.7 billion U.S. dollars in the previous fiscal year. The social network's main source of income is digital advertising. As a side effect from being the biggest social network worldwide, Facebook is the leading platform for social media advertising and marketing with 94 percent of global marketers utilising Facebook in their marketing efforts. The majority of the social network's revenues are generated through advertising – in 2020, advertising revenue amounted to close to $84.2 billion U.S. dollars whereas payments and other fees revenues amounted to $1.8 billion U.S. dollars.

This exponential revenue growth and in year on year profit growth is not something unique to Facebook. It's companion in the success and proliferation of data mining surveillance capitalism is Google [3]. These two tech monopolies what are now command the majority of advertising revenue not only spent on digital but also the reason for the declining advertising revenue for newspaper and magazines. Independent journalism and moreover investigative journalism becoming the biggest causalities in this paradigm shift. Allowing for the development and penetration of a post truth world, where fake news has become as much a part of the news cycle as facts and truth.

---

3 Facebook and Google dominate the app ecosystem.
https://www.businessinsider.com/facebook-google-dominate-app-ecosystem-2017-8

As long as advertisers stick to the policies and rules that social networks lay down, they can run their adverts 24/7 and targeted with such precision that outcomes can be estimated to a high degree of probability. Now we have all become addicted, we will do as our dopamine dealers instruct us. We will go to where they tell us and have as they want us to. In order for us to get our next hit. If your goal as an advertiser is to get someone to visit an e-shop with a high likelihood of adding a product to their basket, it can be so. If your goal is to create engagements and share-ability creating a large volume of comments and word of mouth, no problem. If you want your offer to be seen by more people than your competitors you can bid them out of the impressions each day, if you have a big enough budget. The bigger your budget, the more dominance you can command. The rules and policies set out for advertisers can of course always be subverted. As can the formats in which the adverts sit. This is where skilled digital and creative agencies excel. As more often than not, investment in the creative idea will always bring more value and return than investment in the media spend alone. However this is a concept that isn't always executed well by brands and their creative agencies who are in constant battle for advertising budgets against the media agencies who manage the promotion of content. Both the media agency and the creative are at war for the lion-share of the advertising budget and this often creates great conflict and poor strategic decisions when it comes to social media campaigning.

The perception maybe that advertising agencies are full of highly creative and professional people who know exactly how to hoard and manage big data in a way which lets them create adverts and content that taps into our deepest desires, wants and needs. In my experience this is often as far from the truth as could be possible. The majority of creative agencies in my experience deploying content across social media are extremely naive with the data exhaust and data signals that their adverts create. And its not just the creative agencies. The corporations and brands who enlist their expertise and guidance are just as naive. Naive in the sense that they don't realise themselves that they too are addicted to the very social networks that they wish to command and control with their advertising budgets. Brands and Agencies are unsure and confused about the thousands of metrics that can be obtained from social media platforms, what they mean and how they can be used. They are not shown the details of how these metrics are generated or how the algorithms work. They are only shown a snapshot of the reality in order to secure their advertising budgets on the promise that the social networks will deliver hungry users eager to click on and engage with their adverts. Creative advertising is mostly still all done on a gut feeling. On the whim of a creative director who thinks he, and its mostly a he - there are very few women who reach it to the higher levels of creative directorship within advertising.

Reflecting the biases of the algorithm in reality.

"The time is now" was the title of a short essay I wrote for a marketing presentation in 2016 to help my fellow digital planners and strategists understand that time was in fact the essential focus of the social media. The more time we get could the audience looking at our content for, the more products we would sell. Here are some extracts from this essay.

THE TIME IS NOW

IN AN EVER-INCREASING mobile age, marketers and brands are chasing engagement, still in search of the million views'. The high view digits, significant like counts and plenty of heart emojis - are all the vanity driven metrics. These are not what matters; it's time to be a little more humble. What matters in the ever-increasing mobile space is how much of your audiences time you take each day to understand what this means.

How many seconds and minutes of your targets waking day can you bring them the opportunity to be immersed into the brand, product or story? What does time mean for Generation Y, as the digital experience consumes a vast slice of their working, studying and leisure time? What is their perception of time? What does 'time viewed' mean over a long term prospect? According to a recent Nielsen report, smartphone owners are using no more than two dozen apps. The number of Apps people use has fallen, but more importantly, the time spent on the ones they do is rising. There seem to be limited to actually how many Apps people can use. And that doesn't mean they're not using them. There's an app for everything with over 9.19bn paid App downloaded and a staggering 92.88bn free App downloaded. This isn't going to stop; the predicted downloads in 2017 stand at an impressive 268,692m. I tracked how many apps I regularly used for a week. It appeared to be, on average, 4 Apps, while others ran in the background, supplyingnotifications or status updates. I read my browser; I sent WhatsApp's to my father; I use Facebook messenger and SMS. I check the transport timetable, the map and, regretfully, the occasional Facebook check-in. Each day I easily spent over 1.5 hours on my mobile device. Although my work demands a lot of social media management, a lot of my time in mobile is work-related - but I can still be easily distracted by the content. Taking my experience, I started to look at data sets of behaviour in online video. Both Facebook and YouTube give me lots of time-based metrics to build a comprehensive data set made up of over 12M video views combined. How much time could I take from my user base each day, and how quickly could I amass time viewed of my content in the shortest real-time.

The European Bike Stealing Championships 2015 amassed on YouTube 4,63M of minutes watched, 98% of that happening in the first 48 hours of publishing [4]. This equals eight years and

4 The European Bike Stealing Championships is the best thing you'll watch today
https://www.cyclingweekly.com/news/latest-news/the-european-bike-stealing-championships-is-the-best-thing-youll-watch-today-video-201111

299 days, consumed in just 48 hours. An incredible traffic volume made the content instantly trending at the top of the Sports category in The Netherlands. On Facebook, the video achieved different view results, bringing the combined minutes watched to well over 2M minutes from 1.6M views. Facebook was showing lower retention at 1:15 - an excellent achievement for this network.

With the average YouTube viewer spending 00:02:58 with the content, the accumulation of minutes watched hit a velocity of growth, which peaked at 232,220% of the watched time. A great video can hold a large audience of 3.1M people for 1-3 minutes and more. An incredible achievement from a short video about humiliating a couple of would-be bike thieves. But what do these 3 minutes mean? Well, let's try and break it down in the sense of a lifetime. First, let us consider the Nielsen report. With the average monthly time spent in App at 41 hours. That's about 1.3 hours a waking day, spent immersed in App. Fifty minutes of this time would be mostly Facebook (not including WhatsApp) announced during its blockbuster Q1 earnings report. 8-10% of your 'awake time' is spent within an APP. It is only projected to grow over the next ten years. There are 'only' 2,365,200,000 seconds in an average lifetime. Half of that will probably be spent sleeping. If I can get you to spend 180 seconds with memorable content, this represents 0.0000076% of a lifetime. It doesn't sound like much. Well, let's project this over time.

Seventy-five seconds a day over the year is 27,375, which

is not an insignificant number. Consider this is 7.6 hours. Multiply this by the engaged user base, and suddenly, we start talking tens of years worth of content viewed in just 365 days.

This is significant for brands and marketers. What market share of time spent can you take each day? What does time spent with your product, brand, or content mean for your audience and the development of your storytelling? Where would you like to take your audiences over time, and how will your audience grow over time. Generation X has already been immersed in Facebook's timeline for over ten years. That's 87,600 hours of poking.

Facebook's "On This Day" feature skilfully manipulates this perspective of time spent on Facebook sharing those precious memories' with 'family' and 'friends'. Highly emotive and powerful use of time to keep loyalty within the App. Facebook will surely grow their 50 minutes of the 1.3 hours a day. Projections further into the future would predict users spending over 2 hours a day on their devices as more and more of our everyday processes are mobilised (banking, leisure, search, commerce). New interactive and immersive ad types, Facebook canvasses and carousels, 360 and Virtual Reality, will all compete for the 1.3 hours a day of user time. By considering time as your long term goal and your key metric, you can build your content strategy and storytelling around it. Growing time spent with your content and starting to think about the content within time and digital space. Time and tide wait for no one.

TIME TO DIE

THE MORE TIME we spend on our phones, looking at our timelines the more time we are taking away from our present selves. Time is relative and it is for a human being a finite and precious resource. There is only so much time in the day. So much time in a lifetime. What do we value more? To waste our time or to donate it as a distraction to social media companies who monetise every second we spend on their platforms. Or do we own our time and use it productively for own benefits and well being. I'm sure you have been in a situation where the people in your immediate vicinity, in the same room as you are, spent more time looking at their mobile phone, then they did talking to the person next to them.

In 2018 Ruavieja, the makers of Spain's popular herb liquor spirit of the same name created a video campaign around the topic of time titled #WeHaveToSeeMoreOfEachOther [5]. "According to statistics, over the next 40 years, we will spend: 520 days watching TV series, six years watching television, eight years on the internet,10 years staring at screens. How much time will you spend with the people who matter to you?"

Ruavieja interviewed six pairs of friends and family members, asking them their ages, locations and how much time they spent together. As humans we tend to project time into the

---

5 Ruavieja Commercial 2018 (English subs): #WeHaveToSeeMoreOfEachOther
https://www.youtube.com/watch?v=kma1bPDR-rE

future, telling ourselves that we will always have enough time at a later date to do something. We avoid thinking about our inevitable mortality and fall into the trap of doing tomorrow what we could have done today. Ruavieja argues that a large proportion of our remaining time will be spent in front of screens rather than face to face with our friends and family. When the interviewees are confronted with the hard truth of how little time they have left with their family and loved ones, a strong emotional response is created. It brings a tear to your eye as you soon realise that the present is so precious and that the time we have left with our loved ones is so limited that we must make the most of every second we have with them.

Ruavieja took this one step further and created a website to complement the campaign. You could enter in your own details and it would calculate how much time you had left with a friend or family member. Now the cynical part of me could suggest that an alcohol brand is not the best spokesperson for ones well being and health. Alcohol abuse as a drug does more harm and destroys more lives than many other drugs and substances. However, is our addiction to social media and the time we spend within it more harmful to us when we look at the bigger picture?

Digital well being has become a trend within its self for advertising and marketers. This is most definitely something that Ruavieja and their advertising agency have taken advantage of and jumped firmly on to the bandwagon of being perceived as a caring brand. I will give them the benefit of the doubt that their intentions are pure but their motives are to create salience towards their brand through the use of emotional content which triggers a salience towards their brand to make the viewer feel subcunsoineslly that they care about them and they should spend more time with their loved ones, presumably drinking their beverages. During 2019 and 2020 we saw a wave of digital wellbeing inspired messages from brands as well as the social networks and technology giants them selves. Even Google wanted us to 'un-plug from our phones' [6]. As digital detoxes become the norm, users have started to open up about their addictions. A kind of mass AA meeting has started to occur on social networks. "Hello, my name is Rory and I am an addict. I am posting this message to let everybody know that I am taking a break from social media for a while". Whilst still signing off with the "available on all channels"mentality. Announcing your "break" from social media on social media to me seems like an illogical statement and only an enforcement of your addicted state. You want to tell people that you are taking break purely for the engagements it will bring to you. So when you log back in a day or a week later you can feel proud of yourself that you did it and a bundle of likes are waiting for on your return. Google went even further as to dedicate an entire subdomain to the topic [7]. They then went on through their "Think With Google" portal to inform

---

6 Google and the Rise of 'Digital Well-Being'
https://www.wired.com/story/google-and-the-rise-of-digital-wellbeing/
7 Find a balance with technology that feels right for you. https://wellbeing.google

advertisers and marketers about this new trend and how brands could capitalise on it [8]. A real life Bill Hicks moment if you ask me [9]. Apple and Google both implemented wellbeing functions into their operating systems. With Apple extending this to their not only to their iOS but their Desktop OS as well. You can now get daily reports of your screen time to see exactly how long you are spending on your phone or within your applications. You can set alarms to warn you if you are spending over an allocated amount of time playing FarmVille, watching YouTube or procrastinating on Facebook as you endlessly scroll down an infinite timeline of content until either your thumb cramps up or your retinas go red and start to bleed from the screen burn. Just one more TikTok before I go to bed.

While all the advertising agencies and tech companies were devising ways strategies and creative campaigns to inform us all how we were all using social media too much and being addicts of a substance they have got us hooked on in the first place, something monumental happened which changed everything. The global pandemic of COVID-19. As lockdowns were announced and enforced a large proportion of the workforce suddenly found themselves working from home. Homeoffice would be conducted through online meetings using VOIP/Video conference call software such as Microsoft Teams, Google hangouts as well as the new player on the block, Zoom.

8 Digital wellbeing is about more than just screentime https://www.thinkwithgoogle.com/feature/digital-wellbeing-statistics
9 Bill Hicks On Advertisers and Marketing https://genius.com/Bill-hicks-on-advertisers-and-marketing-annotated

Zoom came from nowhere to become the leading video call software in 2020 with its share price soaring over 382% [10]. The phrase "you are on mute" now most likely being the most said thing in a meeting in the history of meetings. Zoom has also made many people realise that the saying "this meeting could have been an email" has never been more true.

With homeoffice, curfews and lockdowns one thing was clear. People were spending more time online. Not only to do their jobs, but also for shopping, entertainment, playing games and keeping up with the latest news and moreover, using social media to stay in contact with their now socially distanced friends and family. Our usage of social media also shifted. With bars, clubs, restaurants and cinemas closed, a new pattern of behaviour appeared. We started to go to bed earlier. Whereas pre COVID you would see high peaks of social media usage in the late evenings as people shared images and statuses from their latest nightlife experience, the peak of usage now shifted to early in the morning after people took a good nights rest [11]. The further we moved into the dark winter months in the western hemisphere, the earlier we started to go bed. With film productions halted and under lockdown along with everyone else, there wasn't even anything new to stream and binge watch. We started to get nostalgic and watch shows we had seen before or classic films.

10 After Soaring 382% in One Year, What's Next for Zoom Video?
https://www.nasdaq.com/articles/after-soaring-382-in-one-year-whats-next-for-zoom-video-2021-02-15
11 Social Bakers Engage Conference 2020
http://rorywilmer.com/2020/11/zoom-fatigue-make-meetings-great-again-using-roblox/

Funnily enough films about pandemics and viruses were some of the most popular. There is nothing like a real life Armageddon to put you in the mood for some Hollywood Armageddon. If I had to leave a recommendation, I would have to suggest you watch The Andromeda Strain (1971).

This shift in online behaviour and longer screen time didn't go un-noticed by advertisers and brands. The very people who had been telling is less than a year ago to take a screen break were now plotting how to keep you on your screen even longer. Digital advertising budgets increased significantly as did digital transformation budgets. While ad spend overall was down as a result of COVID-19 and the short term recession that it created, digital budgets had increased [12]. An increased amount of content was published to Social Media as well as pushes towards e-commerce stores and online shopping. In many ways COVID-19 did more to advance online shopping and to transform small to medium size business into ecommerce quicker than they had wanted to be or expected to be [13]. The main insight that advertisers were acting upon was again related to time. The more time we spent on social media the more opportunity there was for their adverts to be served for consumers to have a limited choice in where and how they could shop and consume. With the entire planet now forced into lockdown, the shepherds had a more

12 This is how COVID-19 is affecting the advertising industry
https://www.weforum.org/agenda/2020/06/coronavirus-advertising-marketing-covid19-pandemic-business/
13 How Covid-19 changed e-commerce: sales growth and irreversible dependence https://www.thedrum.com/opinion/2021/01/13/how-covid-19-changed-e-commerce-sales-growth-and-irreversible-dependence

simplified job of moving us all through the online sales funnel. Scooping up more valuable data signals and data exhausts than ever before. It had become a complete turn around of strategy. No longer should brands help people spend less time on social media by telling them so on social media. Brands should take advantage of this captive audience and expose them to as much screen time as possible. Zoom meeting after Zoom meeting into online shopping and social media timeline scrolling back into Zoom meeting after Zoom meeting. I guess in the not so distant future opticians are going to have a windfall.

The use of social media during COVID-19 has had a big impact on our mental health [14]. The explosion in conspiracy theories in the era of fake news fuelled distrust and suspicions around the official responses and strategies of governments and health authorities. The more people engaged with and shared QAnon style anti-vaxer anti-masker messages, the larger it grew, a self fulling prophecy within the algorithms creating the feedback loop we have all become so used to being stuck in. The problem was so bad that Facebook, Twitter and Google all aligned to try and combat the spread of this conspiracy. It was too little and too late. The genie was well out of the bottle and no amount of post flagging, censorship and or self help portals within their sites would be able to stop the tidal wave of idiocy that was to follow. Our increased exposure to social media along

14 Social Media During the Time of COVID-19 https://www.psychologytoday.com/us/blog/mental-illness-in-america/202012/social-media-during-the-time-covid-19

with a general mistrust and distain for political leadership had created the perfect storm for dissent, disinformation and it was being utilised as a weapon of mass distraction by those who seek to gain leverage over the EU, US, UK and the Western liberal ideologues [15]. While the conspiracies raged and people stated to burn down mobile phone antennas believing there was a link between G5 technology and COVID-19 [16], brands were sitting back and quietly reaping the rewards of a captivated and screen attentive population. Digital wellbeing had taken a back seat. Now brands would remind you to wash your hands and wear a facemask but encourage you to spend more time online and to keep feeding the algorithm with yet another online purchase.

More now than ever it was time to engage or die.

---

15 China played a leading role in spreading Covid-19 conspiracies; investigation finds
https://www.scmp.com/news/china/diplomacy/article/3121788/china-played-leading-role-spreading-covid-19-conspiracies
16 Conspiracy theorists burn 5G towers claiming link to virus
https://abcnews.go.com/Health/wireStory/conspiracy-theorists-burn-5g-towers-claiming-link-virus-70258811

Social Media And The Seven Deadly Sins

Rory Wilmer

II. THE SEVEN
DEADLY SINS!

Rory Wilmer

Chapter 5

Lust

"Well, she was just seventeen

You know what I mean"

— I Saw Her Standing There, The Beatles

INSTAGIRLS

IF YOU TYPE into Instagram search "#instagirls" it will return over 8 million results. If you type into Instagram search "#instaboys" it will return over 2 million results. Semi naked images of 'girls' outnumber semi naked images of 'boys' by a factor of 4. These are just the images which appear on my direct search of this particular hashtag. There are millions more on the platform. Tens of millions more. There is no shortage of skin and sexually provocative imagery on Instagram. In total over 95 million images are uploaded to Instagram each day. That's about 4 million images each hour.

Instagrams 'community guidelines' state "We don't allow nudity on Instagram, with some exceptions, like photos of post-mastectomy scarring and women actively breastfeeding. Nudity in photos of paintings and sculptures is OK, too [1]." Yet a quick look at the hashtag #instagirls you will be awash with sexually provocative and semi naked females from teenagers to young adults. Many of these "instagirls" go as far to post fully naked imagery and cover their nipples with 'emojis'. Leaving very little to the imagination. There are regional versions of this hashtag too such as #czechgirl, #polishgirl, #russiagirl - you get the idea. Any location with the word 'girl' after it and you will find an endless stream of semi nude selfies of young women. If you search on

---

1 Instagram Community Guidelines
https://help.instagram.com/477434105621119/community-guidelines/

Instagram for the word "girl" one of the first accounts you will see recommended is @nude_yogagirl. Confusing when Instagram specifically stated "we don't allow nudity on Instagram".

Instagram is awash with sexually explicit and provocative content. The fastest way to a million followers is to regularly show your skin. But only if you are a young and 'beautiful' girl. The more daring and sexually provocative your imagery, the higher the volume of engagements you receive. The more likes you get the more dopamine you create and the more willing you become to take more risks in order to make more likes. The most liked image on Instagram, and on any social network was a picture of Kylie Jenner's backside with 18 million likes. Someones arse liked 18 million times on a site that claims it doesn't support nudity and sexually explicit materials. This world record of likes however came to a humiliating and justified end when on January 4th 2019 Chris Godfrey, an advertising creative, uploaded a stock photograph picture of an egg, using the moniker @world_record_egg [2]. The image went on to gain 54.8 million likes, knocking Kylie Jenner's backside off the top spot well and truly for good. The Egg had become the most liked image on Instagram and in fact the most liked image on any website every in the history of the internet and social media. This was an example of an advertising creative understanding the power of the MEME. It was later revealed to have been part of a campaign to raise awareness around mental

2 Egg breaks Kylie Jenner's Instagram record of most liked picture
https://www.nbcnews.com/news/us-news/egg-now-instagram-s-most-liked-image-beating-ky-lie-jenner-n958296

health. Becoming the worlds most liked image did more for the campaign than they could have ever have hoped for. This also tells us something about the wider internet audience. There is a backlash to the overflowing amount of selfie nudes and sexually explicit celebrity endorsed content on our social networks. The wider audience would rather like a stock image of an egg on a white background than to allow a celebrity and her arse to be the most liked image on planet earth. Instagram and Facebook's insistence of pushing sexually provocative content is harming the wider user experience and especially putting teenagers at greater risk. Compared to Twitter, Facebook or YouTube, it appears that Instagram leads to more comparisons between ourselves and others. This, in turn, contributes to more anxiety and depression due to feelings of inadequacy. Research suggests this is due to increased exposure to "idealized" images of other women, couples, and lives in general [3]. Increased exposure is linked to decreased happiness with one's own life. This is damaging to teenagers and especially girls, who are the most likely group to commit suicide as a result. "We found that girls who started using social media at two to three hours a day or more at age 13, and then increased [that use] over time, had the highest levels of suicide risk in emerging adulthood," said study author Sarah Coyne associate director of the school of family life at Brigham Young University in Provo, Utah. Among boys, however, no such

---

3 Exploring the relationship between frequency of Instagram use, exposure to idealized images, and psychological well-being in women. https://psycnet.apa.org/record/2018-15210-001

pattern emerged. One reason why, Coyne's team theorized, is that social media and young girls tend to focus on the same thing: relationships. Boys, not so much. "We know that girls tend to feel and internalize relationship distress at different levels than boys," said Coyne. "This type of relationship distress can -- but not always -- be present in social media interactions. [Girls] also have higher levels of social comparison, fear of missing out, etc. So, that is why the effects were likely stronger for girls." For the study, annual surveys were conducted between 2009 and 2019, with teens aged 14, on average, at the study's launch [4].

The next time you are with a friend and you both have Instagram on your phones try a little experiment. Even more so if one of you is a male and the other is a female as you will see more of a difference. Go to the search feature and look at he recommended content it creates for you. Start to scroll down the endless timeline of content. Make a mental note of what you see. If you are a guy you will see far more semi naked images of young women than if you are female. Ask your self why? Does Facebook and Instagram know something you don't, even about yourself. The more flesh you see, the deeper and for longer you will scroll. Welcome to the world of #instagirls.

While on the one hand Instagram and its parent company Facebook Inc. claim to protect the community from harmful content, a quick look at their search function and the results

---

4 Teens, Social Media & Technology 2018
https://www.pewresearch.org/internet/2018/05/31/teens-social-media-technology-2018/

you will see, paint a very different picture depending on who and where you are. If you are a middle aged man, you are more likely to be suggested content of semi naked teenage girls. As you start to scroll down this endless feed, more and more images and videos of #instagirls will appear. In a blog, Facebook vice-president Guy Rosen said: "We remove content that depicts or encourages suicide or self-injury, including certain graphic imagery and real-time depictions that experts tell us might lead others to engage in similar behaviour. We place a sensitivity screen over content that doesn't violate our policies but that may be upsetting to some, including things like healed cuts or other non-graphic self-injury imagery in a context of recovery [5]."

The figures, in Facebook's fourth Community Standards Enforcement Report, revealed that between July and September 2019 11.6 million pieces of content related to child nudity and child sexual exploitation were removed from Facebook - and 754,000 from Instagram. Over 99% of these were "proactively detected", indicating the firm had still relied on third-party reports for about 100,000 examples. With 754,000 removals from Instagram over a four month period, that is over 6,080 images each day. Behind each image is a real child. Over 6,080 children each and every day being abused and images of their abuse uploaded to Instagram. And these are just the images they found. It represents only a fraction of the total.

5 Facebook Community Standards Enforcement Report, November 2019 Edition
https://about.fb.com/news/2019/11/community-standards-enforcement-report-nov-2019/

With such a horrifying amount of child abuse images uploaded to these platforms on a daily basis, you might wonder what kind of person uses a social network to create and distribute child pornography? What should you do if you see child abuse on Facebook? The problem is big enough as we can see from the numbers they published last year in 2019. So Facebook has a dedicated section to this subject on their help and support pages. It says: "If you see images on Facebook of a child being physically abused or sexually exploited, we ask that you: Please contact your local law enforcement immediately. They may be able to identify and rescue the child. Report the photo or video to Facebook. You'll be able to check the status of your report from the Support Inbox. If you don't have a Facebook account or are blocked from seeing the content you want to report, you can ask a friend to help you. Notify the National Center for Missing & Exploited Children using the CyberTipline: Visit https://report.cybertip.org or call 1-800-843-5678. Don't share, download, or comment on the content. It can be criminal to share, or send messages with, photos and videos of children being sexually abused and exploited. You won't be asked to provide a copy of the content in any report [6]."

If it's criminal to 'share', 'download' or 'comment' on the content, why isn't it 'criminal' that Facebook is 'hosting' the content in the first instance? Facebook claims to have some of

---

6 Facebook Help Center What should I do if I see images on Facebook of a child being physically abused or sexually exploited? https://www.facebook.com/help/189165674568397

the most advanced algorithms for detecting and 'proactively deleting' such content. Yet their own admission in September 2019 that over 100,000 images had been missed by this system and relied upon 'third parties' to report it. Yet it is unclear where Facebook really draw the line. If we go back to look at the hashtag #instagirls on Instagram at what point do we start to proactively delete suggestive and sexualised content created by minors and which is engaged in by adults.

The leading U.K. children's charity, the NSPCC claimed that Instagram has become the leading platform for child grooming in the country. The research was based on freedom of information requests covering an 18-month period to September last year, during which there were more than 5,000 recorded crimes "of sexual communication with a child," and "a 200% rise in recorded instances in the use of Instagram to target and abuse children [7]."

Facebook and Instagram are not alone as being the major facilitators of child grooming and child abuse content. In 2019 Twitter updated their Child sexual exploitation policy 7 to allow "discussions related to child sexual exploitation as a phenomenon or attraction towards minors" as well as to allow "artistic depictions of nude minors in a non-sexualised context or setting may be permitted in a limited number of scenarios" [8]. In the same year UK investigators found that Twitter was responsible for half

7 Over 5,000 online grooming offences recorded in 18 months
https://www.nspcc.org.uk/about-us/news-opinion/2019/over-5000-grooming-offences-recorded-18-months/
8 Child sexual exploitation policy
https://help.twitter.com/en/rules-and-policies/sexual-exploitation-policy

of child abuse material they found on web platforms [9].

Twitter has done very little to protect it users. This can be seen by the daily barrage of abuse which is directed towards victims of childhood sexual abuse. Survivors of abuse who try and use the platform as a means to campaign and raise awareness around the subject, are constantly faced with an army of trolls all of whom take pleasure in re-abusing these victims again, all be it virtually through the social network. It is very easy to subvert Twitter's terms of service and community standards. There is no realtime enforcement to protect communities and users.

Twitter is also one of the few social media sites that allow pornography on their network. It has become the go to social media channel for the porn industry and for adult actors to promote their work. There is no enforcement of age verification on Twitter. Any minor can create a Twitter account and click the agree button in order to view adult content. Within this stream of content it is very easy to find content which is abusive and along the themes of incest, family abuse and underage sex all in the guise of 'roleplay'. You've probably never considered it but Twitter is one of the largets porn networks online with little to no protection from the content. It is all just a click and a search away from anyone who want's to see it.

As well as being one of the biggest pornographic networking sites there is also a large community of users

9 Twitter responsible for half of child abuse material UK investigators found on web platforms https://www.telegraph.co.uk/news/2019/11/10/twitter-responsible-half-child-abuse-material-uk-investigators/

who are supportive and actively promoting sex with children. Paedophiles actively use Twitter to distribute and lobby for the lowering of the age of consent as well as share experiences and tips for grooming children [10]. A 2012 investigation by the UK's Sunday Mirror newspaper and Scotland Yards Paedophile Unit in London uncovered hundreds of child abusers active on the network within just minutes of starting their research. It took national media coverage and police arrests to force Twitter to shut down a handful of active profiles. Speaking to the Sunday Mirror newspaper Del Harvey, director of trust and safety for Twitter, said: "This is a very important issue that we deal with as quickly and thoroughly as possible. When we receive a report and identify it as valid, we take action immediately. You can find our policy clearly outlined on our website. Not only is this a high priority for the company, but I personally understand the scope and severity of the issue, having spent the past 10 years working to combat this sort of content from being distributed."

Del Harvey claims the issue is high priority for the company, yet it is down to other users to actively report the offending profiles, as opposed to the company its self proactively identifying and removing the accounts and content. If you have ever tried to report something on Twitter, you will see how hopeless and useless the experience can be. It shouldn't be the job of the community and the users to ensure a public and

10 Twitter paedos exposed: Vile perverts using social networking site to find victims and trade intelligence https://www.mirror.co.uk/news/uk-news/paedophiles-using-twitter-to-find-victims-1253833

open social network is free from child abuse and sexually explicit content of this nature. It is the sole responsibility of Twitter as a company to use its vast revenues and technological superiority to create a safe space free of sexual abuse, child grooming and paedophilic activity. Evidently this hasn't been such a high priority for @Jack and his Safety team when they refused to take down child abuse content from their platform as recently as January 2021. "Lisa Haba, a partner of Haba Law Firm based in Florida, told The Epoch Times that Twitter refused to take down sexual exploitation videos of her client even after her client showed Twitter the proof that he's a minor, and that Twitter "certainly was profiting off the exploitation of [her client]." The Haba Law Firm, the National Center on Sexual Exploitation Law Center, and the Matiasic Firm jointly filed a federal lawsuit against Twitter on Jan. 20, 2021 [11].

While the world has been focused and distracted by the Tweets of Donald J Trump, Twitter has used the attention to bury bad news as it continues to show its lack of empathy and understanding towards victims and survivors of child abuse and allows it platform to be the number one network of choice for rapists, child abusers and paedophiles. While we are constantly told that the 'dark net' is the domain of criminals and sexual abusers, it is still apparent that the most popular and most used social networks are the main drivers of online abuse and the

11 Twitter Sued by Survivor of Child Sexual Abuse and Exploitation
https://endsexualexploitation.org/articles/statement-twitter-sued-by-survivor-of-child-sexual-abuse-and-exploitation/

proliferation of child abuse related content and sentiment.

How do Facebook, Instagram, Youtube, Twitter and the ever more popular sites like TikTok and Snapchat strive to moderate their networks? They employe vast teams of content moderators. In 2009 there were just 12 paid content moderators at Facebook overseeing the activity of 120 million monthly active users. In 2018 there was a reported 15,000 content moderators overseeing the content of 2.3 billion active monthly users [12]. The vast majority of these content moderators are not Facebook employees. They are contracted and outsourced to third parties. These out sourced employees are paid vastly lower salaries than full time staff of Facebook receive. Moderators based in India and Bangladesh get an annual renumeration of $1,404 compared to $28,000 for moderators who are located in the US. In comparison salaried staff directly employed by Facebook an average make $240,000 per year. The outsourced moderators are the ones who have to review the most extreme types of violent, sexually explicit and offensive content which shared in terrifyingly large volumes each and every day. And these workers face the worst kind of employment conditions.

This isn't just something that is exclusive to India and Bangladesh, where labour costs are cheaper. Facebook has a large headquarters in Dublin Ireland. The Dublin head quarters for Facebook was set up for tax purposes as a way for Facebook

12 How Does Facebook Moderate Content
https://www.statista.com/chart/17302/facebook-content-moderator/

to limit their taxable revenues under Irelands generous tax laws. Facebook are not the only high tech giants to take advantage of these laws. With both Apple and Google having strategic headquarters based in Dublin for the very same reasons. Facebook had out sourced their content moderations jobs in Dublin through Accenture and CPL. During the COVID-19 pandemic over 200 of these employees blew the whistle and complained about the conditions they were being forced to work under.

While the majority of the Facebook employees had been allowed to work from home, content moderators were being forced into offices which was putting their lives at risk [13].

In an open letter the contractors also demanded that staff be given real health-care than included psychiatric care. The sheer volume of horrific content that they had to moderate on a daily basis was having and real and harmful consequences on their mental health and while Facebook was making billions of dollars in profits, it was doing little to nothing to ensure that content moderators where being cared for as a result of the content they had been exposed to. The open letter was addressed to Facebook's CEO Sheryl Sandberg as well as Accenture's CEO Julie Sweet and CPL CEO Anne Heraty.

"Before the pandemic, content moderation was easily Facebook's most brutal job... We waded through violence and

---

13 Facebook moderators say company has risked their lives by forcing them back to the office
https://www.cnbc.com/2020/11/18/facebook-content-moderators-urge-mark-zuckerberg-to-let-them-work-remotely.html

child abuse for hours on end. Moderators working on child abuse content had targets increased during the pandemic, with no additional support... Now, on top of work that is psychologically toxic, holding onto the job means walking into a hot zone. In several offices, multiple COVID cases have occurred on the floor. Workers have asked Facebook leadership, and the leadership of your outsourcing firms like Accenture and CPL, to take urgent steps to protect us and value our work. You refused. We are publishing this letter because we are left with no choice."

"Psychologically toxic" is how they describe working "Facebook's most brutal job". If you want to read more about how shockingly awful being a Facebook moderator is read THE TRAUMA FLOOR, The secret lives of Facebook moderators in America on the Verge website [14]. Not only it seems is the content toxic but also the working environment in which staff are forced to work under. A bullying culture with a high focus on meeting targets as opposed to the well being of the staff. This of course must filter through to the wellbeing of the users of the service. We have become so used to being on a network comprised of psychologically toxic content, thoughts and interactions that we have become numb to the reality that content moderation is a digital equivalent to a sweatshop, where low paid labour is abused at the price and cost of human health and well being. How can Facebook protect the users of their service if they

---

14 THE TRAUMA FLOOR. The secret lives of Facebook moderators in America
https://www.theverge.com/2019/2/25/18229714/cognizant-facebook-content-moderator-inter-views-trauma-working-conditions-arizona

can't even protect the health and well being of their staff? Much like a drug dealer, the want us to be well enough to survive but they want us to stay unhealthy enough to be addicted to the product. While Facebook's content moderation woes have made the headlines, all of the other social networks deploy the same tactics and business models. Where as they all try to rely on an automated and algorithmic approach to content moderation, the fact is that code alone is not enough to determine if a piece of content is breaking the rules or possibly illegal. And therefor an army of content moderators is required to police the ever increased volume of violent, sexual abusive and illegal content which shared on their networks on a minute by minute basis.

Facebook, YouTube and Twitter say they are doing all the can to fight against the issues around the sexual abuse of children and child exploitation, it is surely not enough. While the acts in themself are not a creation of the tech giants, their networks have made it easier and more targeted for abusers to take advantage of. The sexual and psychical abuse of children is not something that is limited to or exclusive to social media. It is just that social media has allowed it to be come more apparent and accesible. Parents unguardedly let their children own and use mobile phones unsupervised. Social media networks do very little to verify the ages of the users and some such as YouTube actively encourage young audiences through the content they provide and promote. In most civilised countries it is illegal to advertise to children. You wouldn't think that if you watched a series of child friendly content on YouTube. A bombardment of prerolls and in-stream adverts will appear as content creators monetise their content created for children as YouTube and Google gladly serve up the adverts to the young viewers. I have watched with my son a popular YouTuber who makes content for children from the ages of 6-13. Every few minutes we were bombarded with in-stream adverts. Ads for beer, energy drinks and dieting appeared. Why is Google advertising beer to children I asked myself? Surely this can't be right. Is their lust for profit so big that they have lost sense of all morality. How hard can be it to make an ad system which doesn't show inappropriate messages and adverts to minors? I wrote a compliant email to the YouTube safety team, just out of curiosity to see what they would say. I asked them why is YouTube serving adverts for alcoholic drinks to my 8 year old step son over-layered onto content that is specifically made for children? An hour later I got a reply. One of those obviously automatically created robot email template replies.

To: legal@support.youtube.com, 7 Sept 2020, 08:26 Dear Legal @ YouTube, Can you please explain to me why my 8 year old son is being served alcohol adverts on your platform? He has an age restricted account and all he does is watch cartoons and gamer channels. How can it even be possible that he is being targeted and served alcohol adverts when it is illegal to do so to anyone under 18 in the country that we live in? The advertiser was https://www.youtube.com/c/KrušoviceCZ/

From: legal@support.youtube.com, 7 Sept 2020, 09:16 Hello, If you've encountered inappropriate content and would like to report it for removal, please help by flagging the video using the flag icon located below the video. We rely on our community to "flag" videos they deem inappropriate, based on our Community Guidelines. For more information on content reporting and removals, visit the Policy and Safety Hub. For more information about our removal processes, please check out this video. Sincerely, The YouTube Team

The reply was obviously automated as it didn't specifically address the points raised in my first email and it wasn't even address to me as a person. You have no name to Google. You are just a hashed number in a big query database. Their reply was putting the responsibility onto me as the viewer to 'flag' the content. The advert was a 15 second advert that was pre-rolled over the original child friendly content. There was no way to specifically find this advert as it was buried deep within the Google Ads system and not a video which sits publicly on a YouTube channel. So there was no way to 'flag' the content. YouTube were also trying to put responsibility onto the advertiser. Yet it is not the advertisers who choose where their content is shown on YouTube. Google Ads system decides on the placements and serves the adverts accordingly to the settings. As I have worked in the advertising business for alcohol brands I know for sure that the advertisers and beer brand will have by law clicked all the tick boxes which indicate their content is for 18+ viewers. So how do beer adverts end up being served to minors, who are logged in on their child account (you can tock box a child's account to mark it as a child's profile) which is supposed to be protected from content that is intended for adults? I replied various times to the YouTube legal email and got nothing but the same automated reply back as response. No human contact or apology for the mistake in serving alcohol adverts to minor. If this is an example of how YouTube takes the safety of children seriously, then I'm not so convinced they have their best interests at heart. Their lust for profits outweighs their duty to care. Even when it's a statutory duty.

* * * * * *

SWPIE RIGHT

OUR NEW SOCIAL media reality when it comes to relationships is that as early as 2011 Facebook was becoming the leading source of divorce [1]. Multiple surveys conducted by law associations and researchers were coming to the same conclusions [2]. Not only had Facebook made it easier for people to connect to each other, it had also become a way to monitor each-other through their news feed activity or more invasively by a suspicious partner picking up your phone and looking at your messages and notifications. Hooking up with old classmates, first loves and crushes were made easier through the use of Facebook's messenger function and the ability to follow someones every move they made on the network. Looking through photo albums and engaging with people, social media flirting and hooking up was after-all one of the main drivers for Mark Zukerberg's creation [3].

The poke button is still active on Facebook after all these years. Yet still no one still understands what it means or what it is for. It always had a sexual connotation and is a marker for the mindset of the horny and sexually frustrated student that Mark evidently was at the time of conceiving Facebook AKA Facemash.

1 Facebook a top cause of relationship trouble, say US lawyers https://www.theguardian.com/technology/2011/mar/08/facebook-us-divorces
2 Seven Ways Social Media Is Ruining Your Relationship https://www.bustle.com/articles/100673-why-social-media-causes-divorces-and-7-ways-its-ruining-your-relationship
3 Reasons for Divorce and Recollections of Premarital Intervention: Implications for Improving Relationship Education https://www.ncbi.nlm.nih.gov/pmc/articles/PMC4012696/

Since the very first inception of 'mass media' people have been using it as a way to try and find love. The first personal adverts date back to 1695 according to the aptly named professor H.G. Cocks. Personal ads were a way for British bachelors to find eligible suitors. According to professor Cocks one of the earliest personals ever placed was by a 30-year-old man, with "a very good estate". He announced he was in search of "some good young gentlewoman that has a fortune of £3,000 or thereabouts." Could this be the very first example of someone publicly looking for a #sugarmommy?

For men it was quite acceptable to make such classified adverts seeking a suiter. For women, it was a different story. According to the Manchester Weekly Journal an advert was placed by Helen Morrison in 1727 who was in search of a "nice gentleman". She got a reply but not the one she intended. The message caught the attention of the city mayor, who committed Ms. Morrison to an asylum for a month.

As well as placing adverts to find suiters, classifieds had also been used a means of correspondence or tales of missed encounters. Throughout the 1700's adverts were placed, mostly by men, calling upon the women they had encountered to make themselves known. Be it a lady you had seen on a train ride, or walked past on the street. Classified ads where a way of reaching out publicly just as you would today on your social media when you make a public post open to all to see. A widely publicised example is an ad that ran in the General Advertiser in March 1748 [4]. It concerned a "lady, genteely dressed," seen leading "a string of beautiful stone horses through Edmonton, Tottenham, and Newington" (now outer boroughs of London): "This is to acquaint her, that if she is disengaged and inclinable to marry, a gentleman who was on that occasion is desirous of making honorable proposals to her; in which state if he be not so happy as to please, he will readily purchase the whole string for her satisfaction."

Adverts like this were most popular in the big cities such as Manchester and London, where millions of people inhabited the cities and it was sometimes difficult to find your suiter or partner. Especially for people who found themselves as widows or widowers and were ready and willing to look for a new partner. There was no Ritzy nightclubs, cocktail bars or speeddating nights for the lonely. If you wanted to find someone, you posted a classified advert.

With this long human history of searching for love in mind, it is of no surprise that one of the most common uses of social media and the internet, is dating. Online dating in 2020 was estimated to be worth around $12 billion. 310 million people are expected to be actively using an online dating platform in 2020, a 15% increase from 2015. This anticipated data excludes potential growth in China. This is a huge industry with vast profits

---

4 Up Close and Personal. The evolution of personal ads, from the newspaper to the social network. https://www.laphamsquarterly.org/eros/close-and-personal

to be made. Especially in Asian countries like China where the population has been skewed through the legacy of the one child policy, creating more men than women. Gender imbalance is a real issue for the Chinese authorities, and the upgrading of the one child policy to the two child policy has yet to rebalance the impact that such a horrific social experiment has left behind. To put it into context there are now some 33.5 million more men in China than women as reported back in 2017/2018 [5].

The consequences of this being that many tens of millions of Chinese men will not find a partner and will not start a family. An incredibly depressing and psychologically damaging reality for them. If ever there was a case for Bladerunner's Nexus 5 pleasure model or a cohabiting hologram called Joi it would be now. However it is not just Chinese men who are looking for love online. The trend is universal and the internet has made finding love borderless.

In 2012 a new player to the online dating scene arrived. Tinder was launched in 2012 within the startup incubator Hatch Labs as a joint venture between IAC and mobile app development firm Xtreme Labs. Tinder works as a geosocial networking and online dating application. It allows users to anonymously swipe to like or dislike other profiles based on their photos, a small bio, and shared interests. Once two users have "matched", they can exchange messages when they both like each other. Tinder

5 Population in China from 2009 to 2019, by gender https://www.statista.com/statistics/251129/population-in-china-by-gender/

originally required a Facebook account in order to access it, as it used the massive amount of data exhausted Facebook created as way to 'recommend' potential dating partners based on your profile and behavioural information.

Since 2019 it was possible to register on Tinder just using your phone number, a direct consequence of the fall out from the Cambridge Analytical scandal that is still unresolved to this day. Tinder started and still remains as 'freemium' service, monetising users personal data, as well as now offering various tiers of in app purchases and subscriptions. If you want more superlikes and the ability to message people who haven't yet swiped you agreeing to start the chat, you can pay to skip that process and start messaging unsolicited anyone you so desire. Tinder has changed the way in which we hook up. People are less likely to meet someone randomly in a bar than they are to meet someone randomly online or on social networks. While Tinder portrays its self as a 'dating' service, it could be said that is also nothing more than a meat market for one night stands. Hooking up for the night and for one night only has been one of the driving factors of the success of social networks like Tinder. Tinder has created a lot of happy relationships and according to Tinder themself "a shit ton of marriages" [6]. Tinder has a very proactive twitter account and has used the method of "tweet storming" as a method to generate PR and publicity [7] Tweeting such things as "@VanityFair

6 Tinder official Twitter account https://twitter.com/Tinder/status/631249399591473153
7 Tinder's Twitter 'Meltdown' Appears to Have Been a Planned PR Stunt https://www.adweek.com/performance-marketing/tinders-twitter-meltdown-appears-have-been-planned-pr-stunt-166351/

Little known fact: sex was invented in 2012 when Tinder was launched." As part of a rant against an unfavourable article written in Vanity Fair which suggested that the age of Tinder was coming to an end because of the high number of users on the network who were in fact not single, but already married [8].

I have my own personal experience of Tinder. In the advertising business we saw quite early on how it would be easy to use Tinder to do some viral advertising to create publicity. I wasn't the only person to have such ideas and there was a wave of Tinder related PR stunts throughout the advertising industry [9]. An example of a campaign I created was to set up a Tinder profile for a job recruiter. Simple enough, finding your perfect match through finding the right job. If you matched with our seductive profile, you were invited to come for a job interview. Writing this now, I almost feel ashamed of myself for being involved in such a stunt. It gets worse. I helped create a Tinder bot, an automated account that would engage in conversation with someone who started a conversation with the bot. It wasn't very successful as users would within just a few messages release that they weren't talking to another human and either just block the account or reply that they knew it was a bot, nice try but no cigar. To innovate you have to make mistakes and only by making mistakes can you truly innovate. These moments in my career

---

8 Tinder and the Dawn of the "Dating Apocalypse" https://www.vanityfair.com/culture/2015/08/tin-der-hook-up-culture-end-of-dating
9 Ex Machina stunt at SXSW has users falling for a robot on Tinder
https://www.theguardian.com/film/2015/mar/16/ex-machina-stunt-sxsw-users-falling-for-robot-tinder

were definitely innovative! Due to this Tinder development I had my own personal profile as I needed to understand how the app worked before making campaigns and bots to run on it. As I had decided that it was now time to stop trying to do such network manipulation and marketing on the network I set about deleting my profile. I opened up my phone and I decided to check one last time on the Tindr app before I would delete it. And this is when something crazy and magical happened.

I had received what is called a 'super like' from a very attractive and intellectually fascinating profile. OK, I thought to myself, this one looks too good to be true. Am I being targeted by a bot as revenge for my own behaviour on the network. No, I wasn't. The profile was genuine. We started chatting first on Tinder but within a few days we moved to talking on the phone and within weeks we had met and were dating. Three years on from that moment and we are now happily married and expecting our first child together. And this was all an accident of love. My wife hadn't used Tinder before. She didn't know what she was doing. Her pressing the super like button my profile was totally by mistake. She had no idea what she was doing. And yet that accident acted as a moment of fate that drew us together and sparked the love of our life. It is possible to find your soulmate through social networks and even more so in a digital world of connections and situations. I had always been highly sceptical of this and especially of Tinder. Yet here I am telling a story of how ultimately it lead my to marriage. The lord moves in mysterious ways.

Tinder isn't all about love. There have been and continued to be a lot of bad experiences on the Tinder network. To many Tinder is known as a Stalker site. The social networks now allowing for even more and intensive abilities to stalk people and harass them. When Jacqueline Claire Ades went on a first date with a man she met on a dating site, it was love at first sight for her. Too bad the guy didn't feel the same way. She was arrested after stalking the guy for over a year and sending 150,000 texts [10]. The messages she sent ranged from, "Don't ever try to leave me...I'll kill you...I don't wanna be a murderer!" and "Oh, what I would do w/your blood...I'd wanna bathe in it." When asked by reporters if she was crazy, she replied, "No, I am the person that discovered love." The charges against Jacqueline were dropped due to mental incompetency but not before becoming global news fodder and the poster case for Tinder dates gone wrong [11]. There are hundreds more examples just like this one. Some of them humorous [12] while others turn extremely violent and nasty. Like the case of Bailey Boswell who was found guilty in the killing of a woman who disappeared after a Tinder date and whose dismembered remains were found in trash bags in rural Nebraska

10 Jacqueline Ades trial: How a dating app led to a 159,000-text stalker nightmare https://nypost.com/2019/01/30/jacqueline-ades-trial-how-a-dating-app-led-to-a-159k-text-stalker-nightmare/
11 Charges dropped against woman accused of sending man 159K texts due to mental incompetency https://eu.azcentral.com/story/news/local/scottsdale-breaking/2020/03/11/charges-dropped-against-woman-accused-sending-man-159-k-texts/5024181002/
12 Eight People Whose Tinder Dates Turned Into Stage 5 Clingers https://www.distractify.com/omg/2019/01/16/h6eZ0aLuM/tinder-horror-story

[13]. There are so many examples this topic in its self could become a true crime book based on social media murders. Perhaps that is the cue for my next book.

The Tinder experience spawned a whole range of applications and social network dating services, all based around the concept of hooking up for sex, rather than dating and partnership / long term relationship building. This new age of online dating crosses all sexual preferences and niches providing a service for every fetish and desire you could and maybe couldn't imagine. Bumble was created to give women the power to make the first move in the 'dating' process. A reflection in the ongoing changes towards gender norms and feminist ideology. "Bumble was first founded to challenge the antiquated rules of dating. Now, Bumble empowers users to connect with confidence whether dating, networking, or meeting friends online. We've made it not only necessary but acceptable for women to make the first move, shaking up outdated gender norms [14]." Where as most 'traditional' dating apps and services would be more populated by men who often made the first moves and often in ungentlemanly ways (sending dick pictures before even saying hello). Bumble built upon the Tinder model. Whereas Tinder required both parties to swipe right to show interest in each-other before allowing conversation to start (unless of course you paid) Bumble allowed only women to make the first move. This

13 Jury finds Nebraska woman guilty of dismembering Tinder date https://abcnews.go.com/US/wireStory/jury-finds-nebraska-woman-guilty-dismembering-tinder-date-73615853
14 Bumble introduction https://bumble.com

ultimately became a literal meat market of men, where the cream of the crop would find themselves at the instant calling of horny women who could summon them to their homes at the click of a button. My sister showed me how this app worked on a visit to Prague. I hadn't heard about this social network at the time and there wasn't much reason for me to have heard of it. My sister explained it to me and I asked her to show me it in action. So she said it easy, I can get any man I want and he will come over to visit me within hours. She loaded up the app and what appeared was a catwalk feed of semi naked men, tattooed, beef-caked and handsome, all ready and willing to accept an invitation for a one night stand at the shortest possible notice. "It's great, they just don't care. They will come and visit you at any hour day or night". I found this quite disturbing, but also intriguing. Was Bumble really empowering women or perhaps the opposite, endangering them? Was this carefree attitude towards one night stands, sex and meaningless relationships generated at the swipe of a button something that was becoming normal to the Millennial generation? It seemed to me so shallow. To act as predators online to hunt down men who are so desperate for sex that they will drop anything at any moment at the request of an application designed as a bumble bee. Was this really rebalancing of gender norms or moreover just reinforcing them? As well as there being networks and apps for heterosexual hook ups, there were many which cater for homosexual encounters. Grindr being the first of such applications with many others that copied and followed. Similar to Tinder, without the swiping features, it would find men who want to hook up based on your geo location. This use of private data would later come to backfire on the company, who had been using the private data of users to create revenue streams without the users consent. Norway's Data Protection Authority plans to fine the platform 100m Norwegian Crowns (£8.5m), or around 10% of Grindr's estimated global revenue for selling users data [15]. In the first case of this size under GDPR laws Grindr is accused of selling to third parties details of users' locations, age, gender and information that could reveal an individual's sexuality. "If someone finds out that users are gay and knows their movements, they may be harmed," said Tobias Judin, head of the Norwegian Data Protection Authority's international department. "We're trying to make these apps and services understand that this approach — not informing users, not gaining a valid consent to share their data — is completely unacceptable." While Grindr has claimed the users had given consent the European Centre for Digital rights claims the alleged "consent" Grindr obtained was invalid because users were not properly informed, and the consent was not specific enough. How can we trust social media and networking companies to protect our most sensitive and often explicit behaviours and experiences. Our need for lust and sexual engagements overrides our sense of trust and not only

---

15 Grindr fined £8.6m in Norway over sharing personal information https://www.theguardian.com/technology/2021/jan/26/grindr-fined-norway-sharing-personal-information

would we hookup with or meet total strangers who we meet just hours ago on a networking site than we would trust corporations to look after our data exhaust in which there soul business model is based upon selling this data to third parties in order to profile us and target us based on psychographic and geographic data signals. Knowing someone is gay and or engaged in homosexual activities could still be used as a means of blackmail and kompromat in many parts of the world and even in our own liberal democracies if people are engaged in affairs and extramarital activities. Online dating focused around the aspects of social networking will continue to grow as an industry. And so will the vast profits these companies make. While we all strive for love and finding a soul mate and or to quench our sexual desires, we must try and remain focused on the true price we are paying for what are often labelled as 'free services'. They are anything but free, the price can be very high indeed.

* * * * * *

OUTRAGED

AT THE TIME of writing, a French film called 'CUTIES' aired on Netflix (Sep 9th 2020) by Maïmouna Doucouré a French-Senegalese film director and screenwriter. 'CUTIES' portrays the coming of age of a group of young teenage girls through their love of dance. Netflix's artwork for the film depicted the actors in their dance outfits in very provocative poses as well as cutting a trailer which focused more on the sexualised dance moves. The movie contains many scenes of provocative dance routines as well as the girls coming of age and sexualised conversations as well as their use of social media.

This created a massive social media backlash claiming the movie to be paedophilic and aimed at an audience of child abusers. Mostly a reaction to the poster artwork created by Netflix in the promotion of the film [1]. This artwork alone was enough too 'ignite the Internet' in outrage, without even having watched the movie or trying to understand its context. What the 'social justice mob' failed to understand, is that this movie is in fact highlighting the sexualisation of teenage girls within modern society and how it is fuelled by lust and all the pressures and addictions connected to social media. The backlash against this movie seems to be more part of an ongoing 'culture war' (the director and writer is a migrant black woman) than it is a call to

1 'Cuties' Netflix Film Causes Outrage for Poster 'Sexualizing' Children https://www.newsweek.com/cuties-netflix-film-poster-children-mignonnes-outrage-petition-1526483

action to safeguard vulnerable girls [2].

As a parent my wife and I watched the film. What we saw was a story of a young girl, trying to find her way in life between two very different cultures. While some scenes were uncomfortable they were in no means exploiting the children or 'paedophilic'. Popular culture bombards young girls with sexualised images of women. From music to fashion and beauty as well as social media influencers. I remember being 11 years old and dancing to the latest music videos which were being shown on MTV. We would learn the dance routines and reenact them in our living rooms and then in the playgrounds. What we didn't have was social media. We had our BMX's and the great outdoors. That was our social network. While there was always bullying at schools, the pressures of looking good and beautiful was not something we had to contend with in the same way that teens do today. We were starting to become aware of our sexuality and the opposite sex. We would discuss who we fancied in much of the same way as is portrayed in CUTIES. The backlash against this film has nothing to do with the film itself. It is a perfect example of how we have lost sight of what we have become through our addiction to social media. Parents will create a Facebook profile for their newly born child. They will upload images and videos of this child publicly. The child has never given consent for this. And this facebook will profile and collect data on them from birth. In

---

2 Criticism of Netflix's 'Cuties' isn't about the movie. It's a cynical ploy in the culture war. https://www.nbcnews.com/think/opinion/criticism-netflix-s-cuties-isn-t-about-movie-it-s-ncna1240165

our ever increasing search for likes and engagement, we have even enslaved our newborn children into the social network.

* * * * * *

CLICKBAIT

LUST ISN'T JUST limited to our sexual drive. There is another kind of lust that drives social media engagements. There is an overwhelming lust for social justice and forms of vengeance that we see play out on an almost daily basis. We will look more at this subject of social justice warriors in the chapter 'WRATH'.

There is also a lust for clicks. As more journalism and media moved into digital versions and a new wave of online only news and media appeared, click bait became an artform. Misleading and provocative headlines ranked higher in newsfeeds through their ability to drive traffic off of social media sites and into the digital eco systems of the publishers.

A trend of quantity over quality was prevailing as new media started to take traffic away from traditional media who were suffering ever growing losses from their printed versions of newspapers and magazines. Struggling to create new business models in which to compete sites like BuzzFeed and StumbleUpon started to drive massive waves of traffic into their platforms, gathering massive amounts of user data which in turn they could monetise and sell to third parties. Facebook was becoming one of the leading sources of "news" for billions of people. No longer did you go to your local or national newspaper to read the latest headlines but you checked your news feed for the most highly ranking stories which were being actively pushed to the top of your timeline. This in turn created a bad habbit. That context of a story was becoming less relevant, what mattered was the headline and the leading imagery. The way in which the newsfeed was designed was to ensure that all content looked the same. That you wouldn't be able to distinguish what posts was sponsored content versus 'native' content that had been created by your friends. This also meant that it would be harder to distinguish between what was a valid source of information and news and what was a biased or misleading piece of content designed to make you click, comment, like or share. All interactions matter to publishers. Ideally they want you to click into their digital eco system, to place you on a timeline and sales funnel. We call this the user journey. Once you have clicked into this journey you are logged and the attribution of how you entered into this funnel are assigned for later retargeting and monitoring of your behaviour.

Our lust for clickbait hasn't diminished even when we made aware of it. As people became more cynical towards traditional and main stream media, disinformation and conspiracy theories thrived. Clickbait has become the tin foil of our social media addictions. Without this paraphernalia it is hard to consume your drug of choice. We chase the dragon of engagements from on-top of the tin foil of click bait. The more outrageous and sensational the posts we share, the more likely they are to be engaging. The more in which we view the world from a polarised point of view, the more likely we are to find our newsfeeds populated with these views. What makes us click more is what the algorithms will serve us more of. We have been cocooned in an echo chamber of tunnel vision, cynical to the principle that facts are sacred. Suspicious of official narratives and more inclined to belive in a MEME than an investigative journalist.

As our lust drives our primal urges to procreate and reproduce, so does it drive our use and engagement of social media content. We are in a cycle of flirting at every opportunity and to showcase ourselves as peacocks on a global meat market of vanity. The more we lust for the engagement, we the deeper we become entrenched in our sinful behaviour.

Rory Wilmer

Social Media And The Seven Deadly Sins

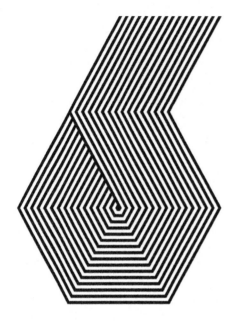

Chapter 6

Gluttony

I'd kill myself if I was as fat as Marilyn Monroe.

— Elizabeth Hurley

CHECKING-IN

BEFORE STARTING THIS chapter, I recommend that you eat something and don't read this while hungry. Because hungry is what you will become when we look at how food culture is portrayed on social media. Or maybe it will put you off your dinner for good?

I'm sure you have all done this. I know I have. You go to a restaurant and sit down at the table, and the first thing you do before even looking at the menu is you take out your mobile phone and look at a social media channel. To look at your latest notifications or to see who is already checked-in to the venue. You want to see where your friends are at that very instant. What are they doing and what are they eating. As the saying goes, you are what you eat, and there is no better way to showcase your superior lifestyle and trendsetting status by showing your friends and followers what eatery, street food stall, cocktail bar or fancy hotel you are currently checking-in to. The waiter comes over to the table to see if you are ready to order, but in fact, you haven't even looked at the menu yet; you've been too distracted by your phone and need some more time to decide what you want to eat and drink. When you finally get around to ordering and your food arrives, you first dress the plate and table so you can create some photography of your food rather than just start to tuck in and eat it. The cliche shot from above, the macro close up of the glistening gravy. The portrait of your dining partner or an obligatory selfie if you are dining alone (but don't want to make it look like you're lonely as who is ever alone with broccoli).

This behaviour is what I call #foodporn, and it can be expressed in various ways. Foodie culture has seen an explosion in popularity, and its rise coincides with the growth of social media. #foodporn had started to become a problem for the hospitality industry. So much so that some restaurateurs began to ban the use of mobile phones in their establishments. Whereas most restauranteurs will do everything they can to please their patrons, our use of mobile phones was starting to impact their livelihoods. Instead of ordering and eating quickly, allowing for a higher turnover of tables and services, we slowed down and ironically in an almost antisocial way. We didn't slow down to enjoy the food and conversation more with our fellow diners or even to read a book or a newspaper as we ate; we slowed down to check our emails, read websites, and consume social media all while creating #foodporn. A glance on Instagram indicates that there are over 255 million images tagged #foodporn. Over a quarter of a billion images of plates of food with a higher than average quantity of beef burgers and cupcakes. As our world faces an environmental crisis due to climate change, we share images excessively of our 'hipster inspired' beef burgers, overladen with cheese and greasy toppings. At the same time, cattle ranchers cut down the rainforests to meet the supply in our demand for beef. While our thirst for rotting meat still dominates tastes, alternatives are starting to appear. As with the growth of vegetarian and vegan lifestyles, the meat alternative industry has made significant progress in plant-based alternatives and laboratory-grown synthetic meat. Beyond Meat is a Los Angeles-based producer of plant-based meat substitutes founded in 2009 by Ethan Brown. The company has products designed to emulate beef, meatballs, ground meat, and pork sausage links using pea and bean proteins as substitutes. As the growth in alternative lifestyles markets turned mainstream, it became an interesting business model for some of the biggest meat players in fast food restaurant McDonald's and grocery retailer Walmart. "Craveable and innovative menu choices" is how Beyond Meat described its new partnership with McDonald's during an announcement of the forthcoming McPlant burger sending the share price of Beyond Meat northward in a "too the moon" style trajectory. In the marketing industry, we describe the alternative lifestyles segment as LOHAS - Lifestyles of Health and Sustainability. LOHAS is a demographic defining a particular market segment related to sustainable living, "green" ecological initiatives, and generally composed of a relatively upscale and well-educated population segment. The author Paul H. Ray, who coined the term Cultural Creatives in his book by the same name, explains that "What you're seeing is a demand for products of equal quality that are also virtuous." A dominant behavioural trait of LOHAS is that they are more than willing to share their experiences, opinions and beliefs on social media. And not just to their friends and family. By showcasing and stating the fact you are vegan or lead a gluten-free lifestyle, positions your social media persona as someone who is actively engaged with doing something to change the current status quo of our unsustainable and consumerism centric focused civilisation. You are what you eat, and there is no more accessible and better way to give an impression you are taking action by constantly photographing and sharing your diet images. Who doesn't want to see another kale smoothie picture from the juice bar at your local Yoga studio. It helps renforce and create a social media persona which is a projection of how you see yourself and moreover, how you want other people to see you in a way which creates engagement. The precious metals inside your mobile phone or the battery of your TESLA car are also finite resources that have a tremendous environmental cost for extracting and processing them. Yet you can balance that by checking into the latest hipster vegan streetfood stall and or sharing an image of a McPlant burger for validation and likes from your peers!

#FOODPORN is a central part of our addiction to social media. It allows us to create and reinforce our online personas. What, where, and how I eat food can create a sense of my sophistication, desires, mood, and attitude. We design and or choose meals based not on how they will taste but how they will look when they are photographed. When you share an image of the food you are about to eat on social media, do you ever stop and consider that perhaps no one else cares what you are about to shove into your pie hole? Expressing your self through food pornography is really just only for you. Everyone has different tastes and psychically our tastebuds differ from person to person. What may look good and tasty to you, maybe someone else's worst nightmare of a meal? Would sharing an image of a chip butty (a butty is English slang for a sandwich and chips are deep fried potatoes) make more or less of a statement about you as would be lets say sharing a 10-course degustation menu from Heston Blumenthal's Fat Duck restaurant? Personally, I'd choose the chip butty any-day, but that's a result of growing up in the North of England. Would I share a picture of it before I ate it? No, I wouldn't. It's just potatoes and bread. Yet, it is a strong statement that has a lot of attitude. Down to earth, real, working-class - British patriot. The latter two of which I am not.

Social media use, especially with children, teenagers and young adults has changed the way they eat. And not for good. An increase in eating disorders have been associated to both excessive screen time as well as the result of consuming social media content. According to a study by the International Journal of Eating Disorders children in the United States who have more screen time at ages 9-10 are more likely to develop binge-eating disorder one year later. The study found that each additional hour spent on social media was associated with a 62% higher risk of binge-eating disorder one year later. It also found that each additional hour spent watching or streaming television or movies led to a 39% higher risk of binge-eating disorder one year later. The more social media children consumed, the more likely they are to binge-eat. The researchers analysed data from 11,025 children 9-11-years old who are part of the Adolescent Brain Cognitive Development Study, the largest long-term study of brain development in the United States. Data were collected from 2016-2019. The children answered questions about their time spent on six different screen time modalities, including television, social media, and texting. Parents answered questions about their children's binge-eating behaviours, specifically the frequency and characteristics of overeating and related distress [1]. As well as binge eating habits, there has been an observed increase in eating disorders such as anorexia and bulimia. As we saw in the chapter LUST, a tsunami of body perfect imagery has put an overwhelming amount of pressure on teenage girls who are most at risk from excessive social media use. Medical and nutritional experts are unified in their beliefs that social media is harming people.

The never ending feed of body perfection focused imagery and content has the direct impact of making you depressed at your own appearance. An ever increasing amount

1 Jason M. Nagata et al. Contemporary screen time modalities among children 9–10 years old and binge eating disorder at one year follow up: A prospective cohort study, International Journal of Eating Disorders (2021). DOI: 10.1002/eat.23489 http://onlinelibrary.wiley.com/journal/10.1002/(ISSN)1098-108X

of "body challenges" has put pressure on people to take often drastic actions to change their body and in ways which are harmful to their health. All for the result of sharing content that generates a feedback loop in the form of engagements. The engagement validates the behaviour and helps lift, if only for a limited time, the depressed mood of the body conscious. Fat shaming was all apparent and even self loathing publicly about your own appearance. The Journal of Eating Disorders found that greater average frequency of negative self-talk "predicted greater frequency of purging, greater attempts to restrict eating and increases in overall eating disorder severity." Dissatisfaction with your own life is a direct result of social media. Or at least the amplification of it is. A 2013 study from the University of Michigan showed the more time users spent on Facebook the worse they felt about their lives in general [2].

The more we try and consume and create content for social, the unhappier we become. The only thing which brings relief is the engagements we receive and thus enforcing the dopamine effect to a greater degree. This obsessive behaviour around food also creates a disorder called orthorexia nervosa. Orthorexia is where you follow strict rules about what you eat to the point where it endangers your health. You strive to eat healthy but in doing so ignore the basic nutritional requirements and calorific intake your body needs to function and be healthy.

2 Facebook use predicts declines in happiness, new study finds https://news.umich.edu/facebook-use-predicts-declines-in-happiness-new-study-finds/

While this "healthy eating" looks good for your Instagram feed, it often does much damage to your body, mental health and overall wellbeing [3].

"Exposure to social media and unattainable body ideals may lead to a negative body image and subsequent binge eating," said senior author, Kyle T. Ganson, Ph.D., assistant professor at the University of Toronto's Factor-Inwentash Faculty of Social Work. The more we indulge in #foodporn, the sicker we become.

Facebook introduced the 'check-in' feature over a decade ago and called it Facebook Places. "After checking in, your check-in will create a story in your friends' News Feeds [on Facebook] and show up in the Recent Activity section on the page for that place," Places product manager Michael Sharon wrote on Facebook's blog. Like most of Facebook's features, it was not innovative; it was a copy of something else. Facebook Places was a direct response to the rise of location-based social media applications like Foursquare and Gowalla, which allowed people to use their phone's GPS function to locate hotels, restaurants, bars, shops and have the ability to 'check-in' to them. Checking in would inform your friends that you were there, and you could save the check-in as another pin in your map of discovery. You could review a venue and comment, and these reviews would help inform other users of what was a hot venue to try or somewhere you should avoid at all costs. Foursquare took this to another

_____

3 How Instagram creates 'the perfect storm' for orthorexia, an obsession with healthy eating https://www.inquirer.com/health/wellness/orthorexia-eating-disorder-social-media-20200309.html

level. As they needed to populate their database of venues, they used the power of crowdsourcing and gamified the application into something called 'Swarm' [4]. Users were encouraged to check into as many places they could and as often as they could. This would allow you to earn virtual badges and gain the title of becoming the 'mayor' of a venue with leader-scoreboards and weekly virtual prices of valueless golden coins awarded on the app. Business Insider magazine went on to describe Swarm as "an incredibly stalker-ish new app". It is these precise gamification techniques that also highlight are real addiction and blindness to it. As millions of users started to Swarm and check-in to venues in a race to become a virtual mayor (for the sake of an ego boost), people partook in the most extensive data crowdsourcing activity on behalf of a corporation. We hadn't seen anything like it this scale before, and it would stay this way until the release of the Pokemon Go application by Google, which has become to date, the ultimate GPS crowdsourcing data grab in the history of data grabs [5]. However, you can't eat a Pokemon. Well, I don't think you can, nor do I think a Pikachu would be very tasty, so leats stick to food-related applications for now as I don't have time to go and catch them all. If Foursquare would have to have had paid for all the data on every location of every restaurant, bar, hotel and shop in the world, they would have paid tens of millions of dollars for it. At a simple sound of a push notification,

4 Foursquare Just Launched An Incredibly Basic, Stalker-Ish New App, Called Swarm http://www.businessinsider.com/foursquare-launches-swarm-2014-5
5 You Should Probably Check Your Pokémon Go Privacy Settings https://www.buzzfeednews.com/article/josephbernstein/heres-all-the-data-pokemon-go-is-collecting-from-your-phone

they were able to motivate millions of people to do it for free, all for the reward of meaningless title and some virtual gold coins. This crowdsourcing or citizen-contributed data became the multi million dollar business model of Foursquare in its self [6]. Alex Sambvani an alumni of Harvard runs a course on digital Innovation and transformation looking into managing digital crowds. Within it there is a assignment titled "Foursquare used crowdsourcing to pivot in the midst of stalled growth, quietly becoming the world's leader in location-based data".

The assignment goes on to look at in depth how Foursquares use of user data was the pivotal moment in the companies fortunes and that the gamification of crowdsourcing and data grabbing generated tens of millions of dollars in capital for the company.

"Foursquare's new crowdsourced business model has opened up many new avenues for data collection which, as evidenced by its ability to raise a large new round of funding, is likely to open up new ways of monetizing. Because of its newfound strength in location-based recommendations, millions of users are now willing to contribute reviews to the platform as well as opt-in to passive location tracking, which has allowed the company to track user traffic. After this pivot, Foursquare was able to raise $45M in January 2016 to pursue enterprise monetization strategies with its wealth of location-based data [7]."

6 Foursquare: Using Crowdsourcing to Fuel a Turnaround https://digital.hbs.edu/platform-digit/submission/foursquare-using-crowdsourcing-to-fuel-a-turnaround/
7 Foursquare Gets $45M And A New CEO To Build Out Enterprise Business https://techcrunch.com/2016/01/14/foursquare-gets-45m-and-a-new-ceo-to-build-out-enterprise-business/

With some much potential revenue and profit involved in location based social media, gamification and the rewarding of data gathering started to get aggressive between the companies who incentivised their foot soldiers as citizen data gatherers. During the South by Southwestern Festival In Austin, Texas, in 2010, a 'locations war' erupted between Foursquare and Gowalla. Both companies pitched up giving away merchandise, organising events on the sidewalks in front of the main conference venue, and hosting late-night parties in bars and clubs. The check-in battle was very much taking place out in the real world, armed with mobile phones and location data, feeding this back into the virtual world of the ever-increasing data centres and bulging MySQL databases. This event happened in March 2010, some months before Facebook announced Places in August 2010. Both Foursquare and Gowalla knew it wouldn't be long before Facebook got in on the action as when something is popular in terms of social media, Facebook wants to come and dominate it. "If Facebook enters into this, and I don't think there's any reason to think they won't, they'll just slaughter everybody," said Alexandra Samuel, director of the Social and Interactive Media Center at Emily Carr University in Vancouver and a panellist at South by Southwest. Facebook dominated the check-in and the battle between Foursquare and Gowalla; Foursquare emerged as the clear winner. Foursquare is still an active social network application and expanded into city guides and creating its advertising system for venue owners called Pinpoint and Placed powered by Foursquare. By harnessing the vast amount of data they had gathered, they could monetise it and create a profitable business from it. With the expansion into Asia through a partnership with Tencent, Foursquare seemed to come out as the winner, if being 2nd to Facebook counts as the winner. In social media terms, this probably means yes.

The habit of checking-in did not come without its pitfalls for the everyday users of social media. If you wanted to check-in regularly to places to convey an active and trendy lifestyle, you could. You can portray yourself as the person who always knows where to go that you stay in all the best hotels or go to the hippest and trendy eateries before they become famous. Or you could just check-in to McDonald's as a way to unlock the free wifi access as you eat your possible meat-free McPlant burger. Yet more likely, you were secretly enjoying a Big Mac and fries. With location-based data comes privacy concerns. Openly and publicly sharing your location data creates a very visible and traceable map of your psychical locations and your behaviour. At what time on what day do you check-in to your local pub. When did you decide to check-in to a hotel, and for how many days are you away on your travels or holiday? In a Hansel and Gretel style way, hundreds of millions of people leave a breadcrumb trail of data behind themself each day as they navigate through their daily lives and openly and willingly share their activities and locations not only to their friends and family but also publicly to anyone willing to look at it. Not only can we check-in to a place, but we can also tag the location of our photography.

Digital photography embeds a lot of data in your photos. This is called metadata. This data is a log of information ranging from the time and date the picture was created, which camera was used and the type of lens. It tells us what aperture and ISO settings were used and what the size of the photo is. It also tells us the location of where the photo was created through GPS coordinates. This way, if you have not disabled meta data sharing on your images, when you share pictures of #foodporn social networks like Facebook and Instagram already know where you are and will suggest the right venue or location for you to add as an image tag. By doing so they increase the volume of check-ins and add to their ever growing and massive database of location based data streams. As soon as the popularity of Foursquare and Facebook Places were apparent, privacy advocates were soon voicing their concerns.

"We recommend that if you're going to use any location identity social network, that you don't tell people where you live. Don't tag your own home," Rainey Reitman, a spokeswoman for the Privacy Rights Clearinghouse, said. "If you at least keep your home somewhat private, you won't be sending an open invitation to burglars."

As people started to have concerns that Facebook would

start checking you into places and sharing it with people without you even knowing a response was hurriedly published on their blog stating "places feature will never tell people where you are if you don't choose to tell them." In a statement, the American Civil Liberties Union of Northern California praised Facebook for taking the privacy of its users into consideration when drafting Places [8]. But the ACLU chapter complained that while Facebook will give users the option to display their "check-ins" to "friends only," it hasn't provided an option for users to opt-out of the feature entirely. There was no way to opt-out. Whether you knew it or not, if you have a Facebook application on your mobile phone, Places would be tracking you. Wherever you went, it would start to be logged within your profile, regardless of whether you checked-in or not [9]. The data exhaust this created would later become part of the overarching advertising mechanism, which allowed Facebook to offer precision geo-location advertising products to brands, marketers and store owners.

By constantly taking and sharing pictures of our food, we have fed the beast of social media while at the same time starving ourselves of our right to privacy.

* * * * * *

---

8 Is Facebook Unliking Privacy? https://www.aclunc.org/blog/facebook-unliking-privacy
9 Does Facebook Track Your Location? https://social.techjunkie.com/does-facebook-track-loca-tion/

ASMR

YOU HAVE PROBABLY never heard of the term ASMR. And why should you? It stands for Autonomous sensory meridian response. To describe it simply, you'll recall a moment when you felt the hairs of the back of your neck stand up. That was mostly triggered by a sound and most often that sound is someones voice. You hear some words or a piece of music or even an ambient sound and you get that feeling. Coined in 2010, ASMR is a relaxing, often sedative sensation that begins on the scalp and moves down the body. Also known as "brain massage," it's triggered by placid sights and sounds such as whispers, accents, and crackles. ASMR videos have become a huge trend on YouTube. Google describes the situation as "the biggest YouTube trend you've never heard of". Now it is time to listen because its not only Google who noticed this trend but advertisers did too. In a Think With Google article, Google calls advertisers and brands to action on the ASMR topic. "Though YouTube is most commonly associated with visual content, sound-oriented videos are resonating with millions of users. Learn how some brands are raising their online profiles by lowering the volume."

ASMRtist's as they have become to be known in the world of YouTube are massing millions upon millions of subscribers and billions of combined video views. The trend is worldwide and not specifically concentrated in one country or region. A brain massage can be enjoyed universally. As ASMR type content became popular so did the subcultures and niches within this emerging style of sound focused video. ASMR eating videos are some of the most watched videos on YouTube in the ASMR genre. Sounds of people crunching, slurping, chewing and swallowing have gained hundreds of millions of watched hours. Zach Choi's YouTube channel has over 11.5 million subscribers and his videos have massed over 1.9 billion views [1]. His monthly updates showcase himself eating massive portions of food, with nothing more than the accompanying soundtrack of the sounds he is making eating it. The videos first showcase the sounds of cooking the food and then follow with the sounds of the plating and then eating of the food. Thankfully he doesn't record the sounds of the digestion and the inevitable evacuation of his lower intestine and bowel some hours later. While you may think watching people eat food is crap TV, evidently by the viewing figures it is not. There are hundreds of ASMR food related channels. Another example is HunniBee [2], her brightly coloured pink hair styles and larger than life lip gloss have a striking and high contrast visual style, making her video thumbnails jump out on the YouTube search results page. She films herself eating massive portion of fast food as well a neon coloured cakes, candies and sweets. It's enough to give you diabetes just looking at the video thumbnails yet it doesn't deter her 6.35 million subscribers and the running

1 YouTube Zach Choi ASMR https://www.youtube.com/c/ZachChoi
2 YouTube HunniBee ASMR https://www.youtube.com/c/HunniBeeASMR/featured

total of 1.14 billion video views.

Why do people find this so soothing and watchable? How can people sit and watch another human being over-eating in such a gluttonous ways while billions of people live in food poverty and are starving? One aspect why it is so popular is the soothing feeling of hearing someone talking in a soft and low tone. It becomes almost meditative and in a world where people communicate more in text format on their phones then they do with the spoken word, listening to someone talking to you in an intimate and passionate way obviously connects with our sense of human interaction. There is also a connection to loneliness and depression. As we have seen social media and especially food and body imagery makes us depressed. Yet we crave to share our food habits and diets as a way of enforcing our social media personas. Watching someone else eat 20 Cheeseburgers in one go, takes the pressure off your self to indulge in this guilty sin of gluttony, yet still get some satisfaction from being soothed by the sounds of it. Watch a fat man eating 10 bowls of spicy noodles takes the pressure away from your self when you want to eat one or maybe two bowls of spicy noodles. One of the most popular internet memes was of a Korean man, larger than life, laughing nonstop as he ate multiple bowls of food [3] that surfaced on YouTube in early 2013. His total joy at eating so much and the simple soundtrack of his laugh and eating the food is one of pure joy.

3 Korean Guy Laughing at his Food + Ice Cream https://www.youtube.com/watch?v=kad8auZo9Ng

I was six years old when the Live Aid concert happened to raise money for starving people in Ethiopia. This event and the coverage of the famine in Africa defined much of the 1980's for me. Out of all the performances at Wembley Stadium in London I can still hear Queen and the voice of Fredy Mercury wanting to break free. The images I saw of the famine from that period were so horrific I can still to this day remember what I saw on TV. The famous BBC report from Ethiopia in which Michael Buerk talked about a "biblical famine". The images of starving children and the horrific amount of death that the famine inflicted. The idea that children on our planet could be starving to death confused and angered me. I just couldn't understand it. How could we allow as humanity for something like this to even be possible within our so called advanced civilisation? Food poverty wasn't and still isn't exclusive to the third world. Many children face food poverty in modern Britain, the United States of America and across much of Europe. How can societies obsessed with #foodporn still be in a position where children are malnourished and going hungry? This period of COVID-19 lockdowns has also had a terrible impact on child food poverty [4]. With many children isolated from Schools, the places where many children rely on to get at least one hot meal a day, more and more people have turned to food banks and food aids from charities [5].

Governments have failed badly in supporting the basic

4 COVID-19 crisis heaps pressure on nation's food bankshttps://www.nbcnews.com/news/us-news/covid-19-crisis-heaps-pressure-nation-s-food-banks-n1178731
5 Unicef steps in to support hungry UK children for first time in its history https://www.independent.co.uk/news/uk/home-news/unicef-food-poverty-help-the-hungry-b1775073.html

nutritional needs of the most vulnerable. All at the same time we waste record amounts of food [6]. While children are literally starving, ASMR food videos are getting hundreds of millions of views on YouTube. Reports suggest that 17% of all food, about one billion tones of food, is wasted annually, the shocking statistic makes little to no sense and just personifies our wasteful and gluttonous behaviour. People are staving while we waste 1 billion tones of food. It makes no sense. ASMR Food Porn is wasteful. It is pointless. It is gluttonous. It is self indulging and only helping to renforce eating disorders and obsessions with food. It promotes over eating and binge eating and often with food that is unhealthy, high in fat, sugar and salt as well as meat intensive. You are what you eat.

The next time you watch an ASMR video of someone eating, if that is the type of thing you like watching. Imagine a new kind of sound. The sound of having a triple heart bypass as the surgeons remove the blockages from your failing arteries. As our civilisations become more obese and unhealthy and diet related cancers continue to rise. As the climate changes and we destroy more forests for cattle to graze to produce our beef burger patties, imagine what ASMR videos will sound like when you are dead. It will be very quiet.

* * * * * *

6 The food poverty scandal that shames Britain: Nearly 1m people rely on handouts to eat – and benefit reforms may be to blame https://www.independent.co.uk/news/uk/politics/church-es-unite-act-food-poverty-600-leaders-all-denominations-demand-government-u-turn-puni-tive-benefits-sanctions-9263035.html

RATE MY PLATE

LIKE WITH EVERYTHING social media, there is a satirical and comedic side to any trend, event and situation. Rate My Plate [1] (RMP) is one of these responses to #foodporn. Sharing images of food prepared by chefs, restaurants and trendy street food stalls are common. So are people's adventures in home cooking. There are some great cooks out there and sharing your home made creations on social media is something that relates to our natural feelings of pride and achievements. You make your own hummus or bake a delicious spongecake, result! However, it doesn't always go as planned. Kitchen disasters are something we have all experienced. From burning toast to more severe situations like burning the house down due to a neglected deep fat fryer. There is a big backlash towards foodie culture, which often is smug, condesending and reflects a certain social class and lifestyle associated with it. In steps the Rate My Plate fans and followers for a reality check and social media slap in the face.

Rate My Plate started as a Facebook group. It soon started to gain popularity and morphed into one of the most engaging and popular pages on Facebook with 2.6 million followers. Users upload pictures of their home cooking creations. Often these meals never seem as delicious as perhaps the original cooks had thought. When images of well prepared and good looking food appear, the audience is often disgusted by the quality of

---

1 Rate My Plate Facebook Page https://www.facebook.com/RateMyPlateNow

such well prepared food. What the audience thrives on is kitchen disasters and school dinner style meals. The more disgusting the images look the more engagement and hilarious commentary they create. One home cook has become something of an internet celebrity. Known as Carol C her kitchen creations have become social media folk law and god like level MEME status [2]. The more awful and outrageous her cooking is, the more famous she becomes. The commentry on posts will leave you in stiches. There is lots of profanities and its definitely not a family friendly page. However it is truly very funny. The kinds of kitchen disasters that you will witness probably go a long to explaining the 1 billion tones of food wasted each year. That's not funny but beans on toast served on burnt toast is, well, the comments on such posts are.

What Rate My Plate shows us is there was like in the case of the Instagram Egg, a backlash towards a certain style of social media content. Fancy food and food bloggers and diet centric hipsters who shared images of food served on slates of rock and other pretentious wares are not for everyone. The majority of people wanted to see and engage with real food. The kind of food that they cook for themselves on daily basis. Chicken nuggets and oven chips, english breakfasts, bacon sandwiches and sunday roasts. Basic everyday food served on normal ceramic plates and with standard utensils such as knives

---

2 Carol C on Rate My Plate is Facebook's biggest celebrity – but people don't like her cooking
https://metro.co.uk/2019/02/11/carol-c-on-rate-my-plate-is-facebooks-biggest-celebrity-but-people-dont-like-her-cooking-8523688/

and forks! People didn't want a small amount of food placed in the middle of an oversized plate with a slash of balsamic vineger reduction around it. They just wanted Pot Noodles and Pickled Onion Monster Munch sandwiches.

* * * * * *

CELEBRITY CHEFS

WHEN CHEFS BECOME celebrities, it is a signal that a civilisation is ending or an empire is about to crumble. The Romans, the Ottomans, and the Spanish all made celebrities of their chefs [1].

Our love of celebrity chefs is something that is reflected within our #foodporn habits. TV chefs reached a god like status and many did that even prior to social media being a thing. It wasn't hard for celebrity chefs to take their mainstream following from Television over and into their social media channels. Like any major celebrity of public figure from television, your loyal following will go anywhere you tell them to. Gordon Ramsey is perhaps the best example of this with his hit TV show Kitchen Nightmares not only popular globally on television, but also a constant meme generator of clips, reactions, profanity and tantrums, which feeds the ever hungry animated GIF loop networks. Not only was Kitchen Nightmares a very successful show on TV it was also gaining millions and millions of views on YouTube and still continues to be watched on demand on this channel. Gordon Ramsey is very active on Twitter. His confrontational and cheeky nature combined with his love of profanity and arrogance makes his persona something that is well suited to social media and becomes an extension and renforcement of the character he has worked hard to build over decades. Ramsey is not going to be

---

1 Four Horsemen - Feature Documentary - Official Version https://www.youtube.com/watch?v=5fb-vquHSPJU

shy about telling someone to fuck off in real life and on live TV, so he sure as hell isn't going to be shy telling someone to fuck off on social media [2]. Let's face it, in his own words, Ramsey is a total c**t! Yet he is also a very talented chef and a good TV personality. This makes for a perfect recipe for social media engagement. Ramsey has mastered the art of creating a 'Tweet Storm' [3]. Be it complaining that pineapple doesn't belong or pizza or that he really hates vegans and vegetarians. Nothing is to trivial for a celebrity chef trying to generate publicity for them self. A Tweet storm is when you fire off a few ranty tweets targeted someone or something you are upset with, while tagging in the media to create publicity about out. In this modern day of lazy social media inspired journalism, journalists are all too eager to copy-paste a tweet. They can create a sensational story from nothing by simply adding a clickbaity style headline that ensures a story goes viral across our social media news feeds. This is an example how social media has impacted journalism and that is something we will look more at in the chapter SLOTH. Gordon Ramsey has built his entire career around the 'bad-boy' image [4]. Ramsey's social media channels are just an amplification of this. His own addiction to media status has seeped through and into his social media and it now dominates everything that he does. He has been influenced by the Rate My Plate style commentary

2 Takeaway guest Gordon Ramsay swears on live TV after promising not to https://news.yahoo.com/takeaway-guest-gordon-ramsay-swears-201900180.html
3 Gordon Ramsay causes Twitter storm after posting 'pineapple does not go on top of pizza' https://www.thesun.co.uk/news/3251407/gordon-ramsay-twitter-storm-pineapple-pizza/
4 The Biggest Scandals To Ever Plague Gordon Ramsay https://www.mashed.com/189247/the-biggest-scandals-to-ever-plague-gordon-ramsay/

and has tended to savage and ridicule anyone who shares their own home made creations with him on Twitter [5]. His savage replies belittle the person who tweeted to him and create high volumes in engagement as his fans and the general internet audience love nothing more than a witty one liner put down with a few swear words thrown in for good measure. Ramsey thrives on scandals, it is the bread and butter of his own style of food porn. He realised a long time ago, angry people click more. And when you click more, you get hungry. Ramsey is not the only celebrity chef who knows how to manipulate social media. They all do, in their own ways. From Jamie Oliver to Nigella Lawson they have all crafted their celebrity personas into a slick and well oiled digital machine. The voluptuous and sexually provocative chef Nigella Lawson can even create headline news solely by the act of buttering her toast not once, but twice [6]. That act in itself was enough to send Twitter crazy and become a news worthy story. This is how ridiculous #foodporn has become. Celebrity chefs are riding on the back of foodies and the #foodporn phenomenon they are active and present on all social media channels. Or perhaps moreover they are driving it and behind it. Their social media content is designed to send social media users in through to their e-shops where #foodporn lovers can purchase their latest books, subscribe to their email newsletters,

5 Twenty Times Gordon Ramsay Savagely Roasted People On Twitter
https://savagehumans.com/gordon-ramsay-savagely-roasted-people-on-twitter/
6 Why Chef Nigella Lawson's Butter Scandal Caused An Uproar On Twitter
https://www.ibtimes.com/why-chef-nigella-lawsons-butter-scandal-caused-uproar-twitter-3084752

buy new fancy condiment dispensers and dress in their latest t-shirts and aprons. All merchandise possible is sold.

This isn't a new part of the celebrity chef business model, what is is the social media funnel and the idea of food community. Grabbing people's attention through #foodporn and making their salivating minds click through to consume the latest recipe for a Buddha bowl salad that looks so pretty on your Instagram feed and creates a lot of likes.

There is another kind of celebrity chef emerging from social media. And these are ones who are not TV chefs but ones who have risen to fame through their own social media channels. TASTY is an offshoot of BuzzFeed. BuzzFeed was founded in 2006 by Jonah Peretti and John S. Johnson III, with a focus on tracking social media and viral content. Kenneth Lerer, co-founder and chairman of The Huffington Post, started as a co-founder and investor in BuzzFeed and is now the executive chairman. BuzzFeed are the one of the originators and instigators of clickbait. BuzzFeed had a dedicated food section and one of the subsections within that was focused on comfort food. They called this series of videos Tasty. The videos are made for Facebook. Short, seductive and containing all the aspects of what #foodporn is about. It is literally food pornography. The Tasty Facebook page as of March 2021 has over 105 million followers. It makes Rate My Plate look like an amateur site. Tasty videos featured all those take away and fast food style meals, dressed up as comfort food and instructed through simple preparation how they could made at home. From deep fried breaded chicken drumsticks to oversize enchiladas and triple stacked cheddar cheese topped beef burgers. All of our gluttonous and guilty comfort food pleasures where being showcased in a video format that was highly engaging and very viral. As the Tasty audience grew so did BuzzFeeds strategy to spread this format out within all sub genres of the foodie and foodporn userbase. The spinoffs included: "Tasty Junior"—which eventually spun off into its own page, "Tasty Happy Hour" (alcoholic beverages), "Tasty Fresh", "Tasty Vegetarian", and "Tasty Story"—which has celebrities making and discussing their own recipes. Out of all of the content BuzzFeed produces, it's Tasty series is by far the most popular, most viewed and biggest source of revenue for the internet media giant. In a two way relationship with Facebook, BuzzFeed and it's Tasty network have taken the genre of #foodporn to new levels and is probably most likely one of the biggest contributors to the ever growing rates of obesity and eating disorders which are directly related to social media use. BuzzFeeds style of shooting food preparation videos, mostly from the top down, with high contrast colour and lighting, no narration or talking just superimposed titles with very basic instructions and quick and easy to follow methods, was widely copied by others. This format worked well and was designed for a Facebook attention span. The average time people watch a video on Facebook is less than 3 seconds. Something we know all too well in the advertising business. If you don't don't grab someones attention instantly, and I mean instantly in the matter of milliseconds, you will loose them and they will scroll on to the next post in their news feed. A method I have worked on for many years was focused on finding out what tiggers "thumb reflex". As most people now use social media on their phones, we scroll at speed through our news feeds through the action of flicking our thumbs up and down the screen. What does it take to create a thumb reflex when the user scrolls down, stops and moves the page back up again so they can view the content of the post that they just moved past at such high speed. What caught their attention and then what goes on to make them click further and to consume the content. #Foodporn was highly successful at creating a thumb reflex moment. What was also significant was that the more in which the food was related to comfort food or fast food, as just generally high calorie, low nutrition food. The user would be more like to have a thumb reflex and scroll up. You can notice this observation in mainstream advertising on social media, how many brands and advertisers also use #foodporn as a way to grab your attention and to be a part of the #foodporn movement as a way of showing how trendy and understanding their brands are. Many brands have created online cooking shows or food related content and they have shot it much in a Tasty style of presentation, knowing full well this content is highly engaging and provocative to the users.

There are many examples of the new wave of social media celebrity chefs. There is no shortage of them. There are hundreds if not thousands of food related channels and personalities on social media. They do get quite niche and peculiar. One of the channels which I have enjoyed watching, as I find it quite mesmerising and an example of how bizarre social media can be, is a channel by a Japanese man and his channel called "runtime [Living in Car] [7]". His channel has just under half a million subscribers and his videos have racked up over 180 million views. He travels around Japan and sleeps over in his Freed Spike Hybrid car. In the evenings he cooks Ramen and other delicious Japanese classics on his camper cooker, inside the car. He is always by himself as a solo traveller and his slow and patient method of cooking inside his car has some kind of calming effect for the viewers. Whoever though that sleeping in a car park would be a culinary event on the scale of one of the best street food stalls you ever tasted. Videos such as "Staying in the car enjoying mackerel shabu in the park at night" and "Spending the night in a corner of a closed campground with no one around" appeal to our sense of escapism in the most modest of places. This is probably even more relevant in the COVID-19 and lockdown age that we live in. I haven't been travelling for over a year. So the

---

7 YouTube - runtime [Living in Car] https://www.youtube.com/channel/UCvIctY0BTwLULhSSpZ6_wmw

idea of sleeping in a deserted car park in the middle of no where actually sounds quite appealing.

* * * * * *

SOCIAL MEDIA DIETING

AS WE HAVE seen, there is a direct link between social media use and eating disorders. We have become gluttonous in both our use of social media and how and what we eat and drink. We need to change our habit as the sin of gluttony is a gateway to all others. The more we feast on social media engagement, the more we drive our addictions deeper to the point where trying to withdraw from our addictions will damage our psychical and mental health. It would help if you considered how you use social media and why. Think of it as a high-calorie type food with way too much salt and even more sugar. If you keep pumping your body of such food, you will become sick, as you will become unhealthy if you let social media use become the driving action and behaviour of every waking day. If you wake up in the morning and the very first thing you do is reach for your phone and open your Instagram, Facebook, Twitter, TikTok or whatever social media channel or app it may be, then you have an addiction, and it is a serious problem. The same goes for waking and instantly checking your email. Please don't do it. Allow yourself at least one hour before waking up before checking your phone. This bad habit of looking at our phones as soon as we wake connects to time and how we now use our mobile phones as our timekeepers. Many people now don't wear a wristwatch; although smartwatches have changed this slightly, people rely on their mobile phones as their timekeepers. They use the alarm feature of their phone as their morning alarm calls. So as soon as the alarm is going off, within seconds, you are opening your social media apps to see what red dot notifications have occurred while you slept. If you start your day looking for likes, you will set the bar for the dopamine high from your every waking moment. Before you have even emptied your bladder, you have placed your brain into motion which will now spend the rest of the waking day needing more likes to feed the dopamine hole in your brains receptors you just stimulated. Limit your use of social media and take a strict diet away from it. After a few weeks of doing this, I promise you will feel a difference. You will have more energy, be more productive, and you will generally feel better about yourself, your work and your nearest and dearest.

Rory Wilmer

Social Media And The Seven Deadly Sins

Chapter 7

Greed

Earth provides enough to satisfy every man's needs, but not every man's greed.

— Mahatma Gandhi

GREEDY

WE BECAME GREEDY. Greedy for attention, for recognition and for engagement. We seek daily feedback from our devices and social media channels to satisfy this greed. The regular dopamine hits of notifications within the constant feedback loop have made us eternally hungry. Starving for attention. The time we spend looking at our phones, absorbed into the social media channels we consume has increased exponentially. The more time we spend on the network, the more adverts the social networks can serve. The more data they gather, the more revenue they create. The algorithm is set to feed your hunger to satisfy your greed; it is tuned to ensure you are never fully satisfied and want more.

In 2012 the average time spent per user on social media was 90 minutes per day. By 2019 this had risen to 153 minutes. An increase of over one hour and a half per day was being spent on social media. Time spent on social media also differs depending on what part of the world you are in. North America spends 2 hours and six minutes per day on social media. Europeans spend 1 hour and fifteen minutes per day. South American's and African's spend over 3 hours per day while Asian and Oceania spend just under 2 and a half hours per day. This is amounting to a lot of time. And the growth of time spent on social media illustrates our greedy behaviour. We just can't stop ourselves. We constantly want more and will sacrifice our precious time to devour more.

Data from the Bureau of Labor Statistics shows that we spend more time on social media than on everyday activities. The WHO estimates that the average lifespan of people is around 72 years. If you start using social media from the age of ten, you will have spent your life almost three and a half million minutes on social media. If you don't think it sounds like that much, let me put it another way. That is almost seven years. To put this into context, you will spend just under two years psychically socialising with others in a real-world situation in a lifetime. We have come to a point where we will be occupied three times more in a virtual social network than in a real-world social network. The term 'anti-social media' has never been more appropriate.

The three social networks which dominate the ability to take away your time are Facebook, Instagram and YouTube. These three networks have a share of your attention. Facebook commands, on average, fifty-eight minutes of your time each day, while YouTube takes around forty minutes per day. Instagram has an average daily use time of fifty-three minutes. However, heavy users of Instagram can easily report spending over three hours per day in the app. There are signs that younger generations are not interested in Facebook and Instagram in the same way as the Baby boomers, Generation X and Millennials have been. Yet they are totally addicted to social media of other types such as TikTok and chat services. They also see how social media is harming them.

Origin released a study titled Meet gen z: the social generation. The study examined the behaviour and habits of what they are describing as the social generation. This isn't some future predictions of what may come; it is already the reality in 2020 that 40% of consumers globally are in the Generation Z category. 91% of males in the Generation Z category use social media. "When we look at Gen Z's near-constant engagement with smartphones, the message is clear: it's the social media platforms on smartphones that dominate their attention. And for half of this generation, social media blurs the line between the real world and the virtual world." While Generation Z is heavy social media users, their mental impact was something they recognised, with 41% saying social media makes them feel sad, anxious, or depressed. The negative impacts they felt from social media use were that they made them feel like they were missing out on something. That lowered their self-esteem and made them feel insecure. 72% said that people their age are too distracted by social media. "Social media reminds me of everything I'm missing out on. A lot of the times I'll find out that I'm being ignored or just not a priority to people important to me." So yet, while Generation Z can identify why social media is making them feel depressed, they still can't stop indulging in it. This is where brands step in to manipulate and control the user's cognitive basis and re-wire their cognitive maps. Creating a 'positive brand experience' is something advertising strategists will lecture to their creatives and account directors. To lift the moods of hundreds of millions of depressed people to synthesise some relevance and empathy towards the brand to become consumers of the brand. Exploiting and taking advantage of people's depression to build brand loyalty and sell more products. This is how the age of consumerism and excessive consumption runs on greed and manipulating emotion due to our social media addictions, which make us depressed.

Feeling depressed? Not to worry, here are the latest sneaker designs that your friends also liked. Do you feel like nobody is paying attention to you? Not to stress, here is the latest funny advert from a telecoms company and you can be the first person to share it with your friend's list. The paradox is that the more brands and advertisers use social media addiction and algorithmic content feeds to their advantage, the opposite effect is happening. People have become quite savvy about digital marketing. There is a growing backlash against it, clogging up our news feeds and seeping into every aspect of our lives. 58% of Generation Z say they are seeking relief from social media. They are at a point when their addictions and unhappiness have become apparent, and no amount of subtle content tailored to affinity psychographics will change their minds. Yet rather than quit social media entirely, Generation Z is still somewhat in denial and prepared to manage their addictions. 64% said they would take a break from social media rather than delete it entirely from their lives. There is hope in the fact that 34% did indicate that they would delete social media for good, but that is still yet to be seen as the rise of TikTok and other alternative social media networks become more popular and could potentially at some point knock Facebook and Instagram from the top spots. As Facebooks demographic shifts more towards an older age group, with Baby Boomers being one of the fastest-growing monthly active demographics on the platform, we have most likely already reached peak Facebook. As its userbase gets older, so will the number of profiles of deceased and dead users. By 2050 Facebook will have more profiles of dead people than it will have of alive people. Deadbook. While this doesn't mean there will not be many hundreds of millions more social media users, the ways they use it and the alternative networks they choose to use will change and move away from the likes of Facebook.

Greed is an essential sin for social media to flourish. Both in terms of the addicted user base and of the dealers who profit from pushing their ecstasy laden likes. One of the main reasons for social media addiction is the business models behind the companies that provide the service are based on serving adverts. Social media is in effect, the worlds most effective classified ads service. Dressing up advertising as content and doing it in a blitzkrieg style fashion. For any advertiser or brand willing to outbid the others, you can dominate people's attention and entice their clicks away from their social media channels and into your virtual stores.

Or, in many cases, psychically lead people into brick and mortar stores. Lead them like the pied piper with the flute play of targeted content. The tech giants get greedy on the revenue created by the advertisers got greedy on the potential viewing figures and measured interactions they could gain from getting into bed with social media companies. Together they have created one of the most intrusive and Orwellian systems that know more about our behaviour, moods and habits than we even know about ourselves.

* * * * * *

VANITY METRICS

MARKETERS ALSO BECAME greedy. They are constantly chasing the high of an elusive viral video. Following the latest social media trends that were always a year or two behind the actual trend of what the internet audience was tuned into. Let's face it; advertisers and marketers don't have their fingers on the pulse. They rarely create original content; they mirror what their peers produce or tailor-make content to win awards rather than create advertising that sells products. They react to MEME; they don't create them. They wouldn't know how to. They reference films and music and books; they don't create them. They copy what they think is popular—mashing up popular culture to fit their brief or brand narrative.

Marketeers hide under a shroud of mystery which is branding on social media. Playing to the ignorance of their clients who know they should be doing something on social media but never really know what they should be doing and least of all why. Suppose you asked any brand manager what the actual return on investment in their social media activity was regarding revenue for their company. In that case, I guarantee they wouldn't be able to tell you. Yet brand equity isn't some magical thing. It influences the value of a company and the price point of a product. What someone is willing to pay for a branded product is always far more than the same item that carries no brand. This added brand value is based on perception. Some extra and unseen value that the brand brings to the consumer. Through social media, this was achieved through the halo effect.

Social media is a two-way conversation with consumers. No longer is a broadcast model restricted to the more simplified sender, receiver models of the analogue past. Your social media channels act as an almost omnichannel experience that forms tentacles like an octopus into every aspect of your company in the digital world. From your marketing and sales to your customer service and your human resources. Some brands and companies have embraced the latter. Especially on Twitter, the ability to create a witty reply or a MEME-like status in a limited number of characters has become a true art form. I see this working best in the FMCG (Fast Moving Consumer Goods) industry and the Fast Food industry. One of the most legendary community management accounts for any brand is the Twitter profile of Wendy's restaurants. They understand the format of Twitter and the tone of voice that is required. More importantly, they get the necessary attitude. Attitude is the most important and relevant thing you or any brand should portray on social media. As without having an apparent attitude, you are nothing on social and more so in cyberspace. The internet has an attitude. This is on display every day in the memes, lol'ing and trolling that happens at a furious pace. Why? People want to be entertained. The internet is not primarily focused on information and learning. It is focused on entertainment, escapism and fun, especially when we are looking at social media. People don't want to be lectured. They don't like to be informed. They want to be distracted by an amusing or inspirational piece of content that they can be the first to share and discover with their friends and family.

The vast revenues generated by social media companies largely stem from targeted advertising. Social media companies collect and process personal data and user behaviour to create psychographic profiles, which they use to allow advertisers to send targeted and personalised sales messages directly to their devices and content feed. This business model and revenue creation have created algorithms that are tweaked to inflate data metrics to generate as much data exhaust as possible to keep advertisers' budgets firmly invested in social and digital media channels. Yet, not many brands and companies can truly explain why they invest in social media. They mostly do it because they think they have to. Depending on the industry and their creative and marketing leadership, it is my experience that CEO's, CMO's and CFO's of very large corporations and brands are highly sceptical of social media and its true return on investment. Without naming names, I recall the words of a CEO of a global beverage corporation saying in a marketing presentation, "We see no return on investment from social media. Yet still, we have to do it. What are we doing that is different to anyone else and why"? And that is where I had to stand up and explain the newly created strategy I had drafted. Instead of using marketing budgets to promote content, we would use it to create content from the source of our staff rather than invest it into media agencies. By building genuine content through staff training and support, we would create genuine content which would have more relevance and resonance with the audiences. The strategic shift was a success, and it went on to be part of a series of changes that saw continued revenue growth for the brand and highly successful social media growth across the globe. We didn't need to pay for likes.

We had to simply earn them. This is where many agencies and brands go wrong. They are paying for likes. They create valid metrics if you earn them through genuine content and don't rely on vanity metrics. You can lead a horse to water, but you can not make it drink. You can't force content to be successful or viral by media spend alone. The actual value is in the creative concept, the format and the relevance to the audience. Humour and entrainment value also goes a long way in this equation. Something alas, many brand managers and advertising account directors are missing. Why so serious?

* * * * * *

INFLUENCERS

THE TERM INFLUENCERS is nothing new, and I find it annoying how the phrase is overused in social media terminology as if it is. In 2018 the term was spotlighted to be the most significant trend in social media. Tracking platforms such as Social Bakers and Hootsuite built their products to tailor and promote the trend. Brands needed to know who were the top influencers and how many likes, followers and views they got to sign them up to become brand ambassadors, as the trend makers and data solution providers claimed that all the buying power was no longer with the traditional sales figures and channels and that younger people would be more likely to buy something from a random influencer than a well-known celebrity or news presenter. This is of course, bullshit. And hype purely created to support the sales of data tools that had the ability to track accounts and label them as influential merely based on vanity metrics of followers and engagements. These numbers rarely relate to sales conversions and are simply pinned on the influencer's perceived popularity based on meaningless metrics. For sure, some YouTubers create content at such a volume and pace that they have a large following and subscribers. When they promote their merch to millions of subscribers, the statistics laws will ensure they sell to a few % of them. However, there are only so many hoodies and t-shirts that you can wear in a lifetime. And not everyone is contempt with the quality of cheap cotton t-shirts with lamented designs ironed that will fade away after just a few washes. Ask anyone who wears Primark clothing.

In Edward Bernay's 1928 book "Propaganda", influence is a word you will repeatedly read. This is because influence is the primary objective of any advertising, marketing and public relations - also known as propaganda. To get consumers or citizens to take action, to buy a product or fulfil a social duty. Influence must be extorted to change people's behaviour. Behaviour change is key to unlocking our cognitive biases. "Modern propaganda is a consistent, enduring effort to create or shape events to influence the relations of the public to an enterprise, idea or group."

The people, institutions, and organisations who had the influence when Edward Bernay's wrote his book were: The TV newscasters, The Radio hosts and presenters and The Newspaper editorials and journalists. These are precisely still the same people who hold the majority of influence today. In the index of channels that impact a purchase decision, social media or online video hold the top position. The top positions are held by TV, Radio, Film, Newspapers and Magazines. Social media and digital channels come in around 7th in the rankings. What I am saying may seem controversial in the digital age. However, we still live in an omnichannel world where communication and messaging take all forms in both the physical and digital world. All that has changed is the frequency and the level of bombardment we are constantly under siege from. This high volume, or frequency as we call it, of messaging and advertisements has become so prevalent that our brains have evolved to develop inbuilt ad blockers. We recognise an advert wherever we see it. Be it a billboard along the highway or draped across the front of a big building. Be it a banner advert on a website or a piece of content designed to look like an original post by our friends on our social media timelines. We skip the ad after five seconds. If it lasts longer than five seconds, we might even turn off and forgo watching the original video because of the advertisement's intrusion. Savvy technical users know how to install ad blockers into their browser and on their computers to block adverts, but the majority of us make use of our inbuilt ad blocker, which our brains have developed all by themselves.

THE BACKLASH BEGINS

INFLUENCERS PERSONIFY GREED. Greed is the primary motivation for their gain. They were acting as surrogates for brands and advertising, trying to persuade the masses to consume more. Influencer greed has reached its peak in 2019 and into 2020. There has now started to be a genuine backlash against influencer personalities. Whereas "social media consultancies" and "social data trends agencies" had been espousing the notion of "Influencer Marketing" for some years to sell their simplistic data insights, they were very out of touch with how the real audiences and everyday people felt. As the world went into strict COVID-19 lockdowns and travel restrictions were put into place, the only saving grace would be that "travel bloggers and travel influencers" would have nothing more to do and say. At last, a timeline free of travel influencer marketing.

Elle Darby was from the UK and described herself as a 'social media influencer' with as little a following as eighty-seven thousand YouTube subscribers and seventy-six thousand Instagram followers. There are inanimate objects with more followers on Instagram than that. Non the less it didn't stop the 22-year-old from using her social media following to try and demand five nights free stay at a luxury five-star hotel, The White Moose Cafe in Dublin.

Ms Darby wrote an email to the hotel stating, "I work as a social media influencer, mainly lifestyle, beauty & travel based. My partner and I are planning to come to Dublin for an early Valentine's Day weekend from Feb 8th to 12th to explore the area. As I was searching for places to stay, I came across your stunning hotel and would love to feature you in my YouTube videos/dedicated Instagram stories/posts to bring traffic to your hotel and recommend others to book up in return for free accommodation."

The White Moose Cafe didn't take kindly to her requests

and decided to use their social media to respond publicly. Writing on their Facebook page, they replied. "Dear Social Influencer (I know your name but apparently, it's not important to use names. Thank you for your email looking for free accommodation in return for exposure. It takes a lot of balls to send an email like that, if not much self-respect and dignity. If I let you stay here in return for a feature in a video, who is going to pay the staff who look after you? Who is going to pay the housekeepers who clean your room? The waiters who serve you breakfast? The receptionist who checks you in? Who is going to pay for the light and heat you use during your stay? Maybe I should tell my staff they will be featured in your video in lieu of receiving payment for work carried out while you're in residence?". The message concludes: "P.S. The answer is no."

The post went viral, gaining mainstream attention and thousands of messages of support from the general public and other hospitality business many who were also fed up with the greed of so-called influencers. Ms Darby was so upset by the rejection and humiliation that she took to her YouTube channel and uploaded a 17-minute tearful video describing her humiliation, embarrassment and anger. The video has since been removed and deleted by Ms Darby but not before it was shared globally by mass media news outlets. Ms Darby had become a global influencer - if only to become the poster child representing the backlash against influencer marketing and influencer lifestyles.

WHEN INFLUENCING BECOMES DEADLY

The stakes for Influencers have become deadly. In the ever-increasing war for attention and likes, social media influencers are constantly trying to create new content types that increase viewers and followers. Just like the social networks that host them, influencers are concerned only with growth. The next follower milestone. The next million views. This behaviour has become fatal and carries high risks.

Ekaterina Didenko is from Russia and is a famous blogger and Instagrammer with over one million followers. The mother-of-two is a highly qualified pharmacist and gave advice to her followers on keeping home medicine cupboards. She had support from the pharmaceutical industry and would review over the counter medicines and blog about her life as a mother and an influencer. On her 29th birthday a tragic accident occurred at a spa in the south of Moscow in February 2020 [1]. The incident was of course, live-streamed on her social media in real-time. As Ekaterina and a large group of her friends clinked glasses standing around a swimming pool, her husband Valentin Didenko unloaded 55lbs of dry ice into the pool. His intention was to create a dramatic effect to impress the guests and the watching social media audience. As the dry ice reacted with the water, Valentin and others jumped into the pool, creating heavy vapour.

---

1 Three people dead after dry ice tragedy at blogger's birthday party https://au.news.yahoo.com/dry-ice-tragedy-kills-three-ekaterina-didenko-birthday-party-084837903.html

What they hadn't realised, and is somewhat confusing as to why qualified pharmacists and engineers wouldn't have considered it, the reaction of dry ice and water created a tremendous amount of carbon dioxide. Valentin, Ekaterina and other guests were rushed to intensive care. Suffering from carbon dioxide poisoning and chemical burns. Two of the guests were pronounced dead at the scene, while Valentin died in the hospital. Miraculously Ekaterina survived. Her stupidity in search of engagement had cost her the life of her husband as well as two of her friends. Strangely, rather than withdrawing from social media, Ekaterina took to social media to create live Instagram stories to express her grief and loss within hours of the tragic event ending in death. This saw her social media followers soar by over half a million more within a day. As her followers increased, so did the volume of videos and posts she created. Rather than mourn in private, Ekaterina used the incident to continue the growth in her social media channels and harvest engagements. Many news outlets and bloggers in Russia slammed Ekaterina for being immoral. How could she be so vain as to continue to make social media posts in such a short time after the event? It was described as "broadcasting from morgue". Ekaterina also used her suffering children in her social media broadcasts. She gave her four-year-old daughter a doll in an Instagram video, saying it was from her late father. "Who gave you this doll?" Ekaterina asked her daughter, who replied: 'Daddy.' Ekaterina asked her: 'And how did you call her, tell us?', to which she replied: "Valentina" (named after her father).

We can be in no doubt the incident is tragic, and the loss of all concerned is horrific; we can't ignore Ekaterina's behaviour and how she couldn't stop herself from continuing to broadcast on social media even in the face of such loss. A pointless and totally avoidable series of deaths that only occurred due to the desire and objective to create a visual effect for her social media videos. The authorities in Russia opened an investigation and confirmed a criminal case would be opened for causing death by negligence. If you look at Ekaterina's Instagram today, you wouldn't even think that she had been through such a tragedy. Her following has grown to 1.7 million followers and she posts pictures of her self on exotic beaches, in fashionable clothing and picture perfect images of her family [2]. While she often posts images of herself and Valentina to remind her new followers of her infamous status, she seems undeterred in how she uses social media to promote a very image controlled view of her life and her success as a pharmacists mother and influencer.

Ekaterina isn't a lone example of death by negligence for the sake of social media engagement. The innocent 'selfie' has also started to become a cause of death for influencers trying to go one further than anyone else in their addiction for engagement. In January 2019, a 21-year-old Instagram model died after falling from a cliff in. Originally from the UK, Madalyn Davis climbed over a fence at a selfie-hotspot in Diamond Bay,

2 Instagram @didenko.katerina https://www.instagram.com/didenko.katerina/

Australia. Whilst trying to create a selfie, she slipped and fell 262 feet and was found dead at a depth of 55 feet below the ocean surface.

After a post mortem toxicology report coroners found that Madalyn was highly intoxicated with alcohol with traces of amphetamines, cocaine, ketamine, and MDMA [3]. She had left a house party to climb over the fence to make a 'sunrise selfie'. While obviously, her altered state of mind played a big part in her poor decision-making, the greed for more likes and engagements was irresistible at having the opportunity to make a 'perfect selfie'. Is life worth more likes on Instagram? Which drug really killed her? The alcohol and MDMA or the dopamine hit from a social media like?

While it may seem easy to mock the tragic deaths of people like Madalyn Davis and Ekaterina Didenko's husband and friends, it is an ever-increasing fact that more and more people are willing to take hazardous and fatal risks to create engaging or trending social media content. Daredevils and free climbing buildings illegally are a massive trend on Instagram, Facebook, and YouTube. The trend is to break into a building site of a new building or scale a well-known high storey building and/ or landmark. It could be the Shard tower in London or a cooling tower chimney stack. It doesn't really matter what the structure is, as long as it is high and there is an element of breaking and entry

---

3 Sydney 'selfie hotspot' death Briton Madalyn Davis 'took drugs' https://www.bbc.com/news/uk-england-lincolnshire-55401817

involved. With the development of cameras like GoPro, people have been told to be 'Hero's' and challenged to do more daring and white knuckle style stunts on top of skyscrapers. GoPro even use such stunts and footage in their promotional content [4]. This ability to film in high definition with small, lightweight cameras designed for stunts and extreme sports has spurred on an ever willing number of risk-takers. The resulting content is sure to gain millions of views and high engagements from a ready and willing audience who like nothing more than to see people take risks and either fail, fall or win at the challenges as they become more and more extreme in the name of being heroic.

Jason Coe was just 25 when his body was found at the base of a building [5]. The daredevil had been performing backflips on top of the skyscraper to create content for his Instagram channel. Jason Coe had a modest amount of followers, so it can be said he did what he did just for its fame, yet he still put his life on the line to make content for his social media channels. In one of his posts a comment reported to be from his mother wrote "What the hell are you doing?" to which he replied "Hahaha just on a roof" [6]. There are now many examples of how creating social media content has lead to deaths it has coined the term "selficide". The Bikini Hiker from Taiwan, Gigi Wu fell into a

4 GoPro: Skyscraper Handstand in Tel Aviv with Jason Paul https://www.youtube.com/watch?v=mhNnxwRJ8Cs
5 Man who fell to his death was thrill-seeker who shared snaps of his adventures on social media https://www.foxnews.com/us/man-who-fell-to-his-death-was-thrill-seeker-who-shared-snaps-of-his-adventures-on-social-media
6 Instagram @jcoe210 https://www.instagram.com/jcoe210/

ravine whilst hiking through Yushan National Aprk [7]. The injuries from her fall didn't kill her but the hyperthermia did. A Chinese 'superman' and acclaimed 'rooftopper' Wu Yongnin plunged to his death whilst scaling the sixty-two storey Huayuan Hua building, without any safety equipment [8]. He was filming the stunt on order to gain sponsorship from a brand to fund his stunts for his sixty-thousand followers. A seventeen-year-old in Mumbai drowned whilst trying to create a perfect selfie [9]. As Priti Pise perched on rocks trying to create the perfect frame for his shot, he slipped and lost his balance. The strong waves dragged him deeper out to sea, and he lost his life.

Our greed for engagement is killing us. Our greed for consuming social media content is killing others. Is the price of life truly worth paying for likes, shares and video views? Is social media becoming nothing more than an opportunity to create and distribute snuff videos? From live streaming of murders and accidental deaths to the daredevils and risk-takers who encounter near misses and brush with death each day. When does our greed become deadly, and how do we stop our addiction to always wanting more.

* * * * * *

---

7 Gigi Wu, Taiwanese 'bikini hiker,' dies after mountain fall https://www.cnn.com/2019/01/22/asia/taiwan-gigi-wu-death-intl/index.html

8 Wu Yongning: Who is to blame for a daredevil's death? https://www.bbc.com/news/world-asia-china-42335014

9 Mumbai boy drowns while taking selfie with friend at Marine Drive https://indianexpress.com/article/cities/mumbai/mumbai-boy-drowns-while-taking-selfie-with-friend-at-marine-drive-5220695/

MEME STONKS & SOCIAL TRADING

DURING 2007 - 2008 THE GLOBAL financial markets crashed. Instigated by the subprime mortgage crisis and the subsequent bursting of the housing market bubble. The trouble started in the United States and quickly spread to financial institutions all across the world. As the reality of the situation sunk in, we became shocked at the greed of the banks and bankers and how ultimately they were bailed out by taxpayers money only to reward themselves with huge bonuses and increased salaries. We all knew that greed was a product of banking and spread wildly on the trading floors of Wall Street as in all stock exchanges around the world. Greed is an essential part of consumer capitalism. Without greed, there is no growth. You have to keep wanting more, even to the point of self-destruction. Five years after the financial crisis in 2013, a Hollywood movie hit our screens with much acclaim. The Wolf of Wall Street, directed by Martin Scorsese and written by Terence Winter. The film starred Leonardo DiCaprio in the leading role-playing the real-life character of Jordan Belfort, to which the film was based on his biography by the same title. Belfort's biography and Winter's screenplay recounts Belfort's account of his career as a stockbroker in New York City and how his firm, Stratton Oakmont, engaged in rampant corruption and fraud on Wall Street led to his downfall.

The film grossed over $392 million worldwide during its theatrical run and was a huge success. Audiences loved nothing more than following the sordid tales of Belfort and his hard drugs and high-class hooker lifestyle. Audiences related to greed. Far from being put off from the idea of Wall Street Traders and Bankers, the very people who had taken us to the brink of civilisation as we know, they cherished and applauded the portrayal of greed. There is a Wolf of Wallstreet within us all. Animated GIFS and lines from the movie soon became internet folk law with an entire subsection of MEMEs created from moments in the film and the lines delivered by DiCaprio. Rather than make a movie that showcased the very worst of human nature, Scorsese had created a MEME monster that would go on to inspire millions of people to gamble their money away on social trading sites like Robin Hood and eToro.

A year before the release of The Wolf of Wallstreet, Jaime Rogozinski, an entrepreneur living in Washington, D.C, decided to create a subreddit on the popular social media message board, Reddit. In January 2012, Rogozinski became the creator and moderator of /r/wallstreetbets. A subreddit dedicated to stock trading and stock speculation as a way of boasting about trading profits as well as talking about trading failures. The initial motto of the subreddit as a sign for what would come was "Inspired by earnings seasons. Let's play." Wall Street Bets or WSB as it has become known, started of small, as a niche group of a few users who posted insights and their experiences with the stock market. These were high street traders and not the giant Whales of Wall Street and the megabank hedge funds. Just everyday entrepreneurs and investors looking for the next penny stock or big tech bubble could propel them to Warren Buffet like portfolios. What united them all is that they wanted to be wealthy, and they were greedy. The risk was worth taking for the potential payback. If you lost it all, at least you had a good post you could share with the group, and everyone would laugh with you and cry at the same time. By 2013 WSB was still a tiny and somewhat unorganised group of Redditers. In April 2013, a new application and was created which aimed to change stock trading for good. The company Robin Hood was founded in the San Francisco bay area. Initially, as just a way to track stocks, but the aim of the company was to become an online brokerage with no commissions. It aimed to target young investors and be a 'mobile only' trading platform, favouring the types of people who frequented Reddit and the Wallstreetbets subreddit. By October of 2013, Robin Hood had been approved by the Financial Industry Regulatory Authority approved it to act as a stock brokerage. At the same in Israel, a Tel Aviv start-up called eToro was gaining tens of millions of dollars in investment from venture capitalists. It too was set up to be a stock brokerage firm, with so-called no fees and no commission. It also had another feature: it would act as a social trading network, a Facebook-style stockbroker, allowing users to follow, comment, and copy other traders. If you saw someone was making great trades, all you had to do was invest some money and hit the copy trade button. You didn't have to know anything about the stock market or trading; you could just let someone else do it for you. What both companies have in common was a business model which is based on a lie. They both suggest there is no fee or no commission; it is not accurate and very misleading. There is a fee and a very high one, it is called 'the spread'. The price at which the companies sell you the stock is not the price to buy the stock. The percentage difference is called the spread, and it is how both of these companies started to created revenues and profits of hundreds of millions of dollars. Charlie Munger, vice chairman of Berkshire Hathaway and long-time business partner of Warren Buffett, said that no-commission trading business models were "a dirty way to make money." Munger was being asked about the most egregious excesses in the financial system and named Robinhood by name. "Well, it's most egregious in the momentum trading by novice investors lured in by new types of brokerage operations like Robinhood," he said. "And I think all of this activity is regrettable. I think civilisation would be better without it. It's really stupid to have a culture that encourages as much gambling in stocks by people who have the mindset of racetrack bettors. And of course, it's going to create trouble, as it did,"

Munger was right; it had caused a lot of trouble and

encouraged a lot of greed. So how did we get to the point where one of the most successful hedge fund managers was speaking out in such ways against the social trading companies? These mobile trading apps had encouraged and enabled everyday people to trade stocks from the comfort of their homes with the ease of a mobile phone application?

Between 2014 and 2015 Wallstreetbets subreddit still wasn't so significant as far as membership of subreddits goes. It had hit the 5,000 member mark in February 2014 and continued to grow but at a rather sluggish pace. Within a year, a new phrase and social media philosophy and hashtag had started to become popular. #YOLO stands for You Only Live Once, and it was being used as a catchall attitude hashtag for a millennial generation. A generation who were more than willing to take risks in return for material and social media kudus gain. The more you # YOLO'd, the more engagement you could get when you shared your story with others. If you # YOLO'd and became filthy rich, your story would become viral. If you # YOLO'd and failed miserably, your story would still become viral. It was a win-win attitude to have. No matter how it ended up, you were guaranteed some payback in social media engagement.

Robinhood and eToro were starting to become top-rated apps and services. June 2015 and Robinhood was awarded an Apple Design Award, and in 2016, Google awarded them another design award. Their apps were driving millions of downloads and enabling everyday people the ability to trade stocks and become their very own little Wolfs of Wallstreet. Or should we say Foxes of the High Street? The scene was now set for what would unfold in late 2020 and early 2021.

We fast forward to today. 'Wallstreetbets' subreddit now has over 9.6 million members, and Robinhood is being investigated by the financial securities commissions. eToro is about to go public via a SPAC merger in a $10B deal. The COVID-19 pandemic caused the stock market to fall drastically at the start of the outbreak. This drop in prices encouraged millions of amateur investors to start to use Robinhood and eToro trading apps. This influx of money and inexperienced users causes the market to rally. Deutsche Bank analyst Parag Thatte points to Robinhood trader data to show that institutional investors are chasing amateur investors. The Wolf of Wallstreet is now pursuing the Fox of the Highstreet. 'Wallstreetbets' and its #YOLO attitude, with a handful of selected stocks, had been given the label of "MEME-STATUS" and on a trajectory "TO THE MOON." One of these MEME stocks was the company GameStop ($GME).

You had probably not heard of the Reddit user called 'Roaring Kitty' unless you were a member of the subreddit Wallstreetbets. 'Roaring Kitty' shot to Reddit God-like status when his long term investment and belief in GameStop ($GME) came to a dazzling all-time high thanks to the YOLO brotherhood of Wallstreetbets members. 'Roaring Kitty' probably never thought that he would one day find himself on a Zoom call giving remote evidence to a confessional hearing into the trading activities of Robin Hood and the $GME stock trading meltdown. Some people claimed it had partly happened as a result of his speculations on Reddit. As the $GME stock started to rise rapidly, the mainstream media began to promote it. In turn, it created a cascade of thousands if not hundreds of thousands of high street traders using mobile trading apps to jump on the bandwagon and invest their life savings into the stock. Many people even took out loans to buy stock, and many bought stock using leverage. A massive mistake. As obviously, as soon as the stock had risen to its ATH (all-time high), the bubble burst and the stock price came crashing down again, leaving many of the individual high street investors out of pocket, having lost the value of everything they had just invested. This is the purest example of GREED which is amplified by social media. The idea that you could get rich quick through one fast investment and become a multimillionaire overnight. Look 'Roaring Kitty' on paper. He had become a multimillionaire from his investment in $GME. Yet just as quickly as his fortune had amassed, it had been lost. Social Media sites and Trading App users were encouraging as many people to buy and hold $GME stock so they could bankrupt the hedge funds which had been betting against $GME stock and short-selling it. Social media users were big-upping each other up and telling each other to hold firm and not sell their stock and that the stock would keep rising the longer they hold it. Of course, this didn't happen, as the $GME was so incredibly overvalued and not reflective of the profit and product sales of the company. GameStop is a brick and mortar video game store. In an age where mostly all new games are downloaded through online stores, the amount of debt owed by the company and the prospects of turning around the brick and mortar gaming industry seemed futile by all analysis, a terrible investment. Yet this is what the YOLO and Wallstreetbets were all about. To find the underdog stock and bet against the hedge fund short sellers in a David and Goliath battle for great fortune. No doubt many savvy traders will have been able to flip the GameStop Reddit story in their favour and would have managed to day trade a very handsome profit, and I am sure many traders will have sold out while the stock reached its all-time highs. However, the majority of the high street traders didn't, and they lost their children's college funds in the process. Social media stock trading leads to the amplification of greed. Investing in the stock market is not a quick gain, quick-win process unless you are a highly skilled and highly experienced trader with a vast array of assets and investments at your disposal. For the everyday high street trader using their mobile phone to buy and sell shares, you should be thinking long term and small but steady increments of profit. Combined with an intelligent use and reinvestment of compound interest, you might find yourself in ten years or more owning a nice little nest egg. If your aim is to try and make money fast, then I would suggest you have far better odds just going to a casino than you have gambled on the stock market with the so-called "free trading apps". There is no such thing as a free lunch, and these apps are far from free. The 'spread' is the fee and what you buy and sell the shares at is fractionally higher or lower than the actual market rate. You are paying well over the odds for trading, and the only winners in this game are the companies like Robin Hood and eToro, who profit from our amplified sense of greed through our abuse of social media. As they write on all the trading websites and in the small print of the terms and conditions of the apps: This is not investment advice. Never invest more than you can afford to lose.

* * * * * *

PROFIT OVER PEOPLE

WE HAVE ALL become too greedy. Greedy for likes, shares and attention. Spending most of our waking days staring into our mobile phone screens. Oblivious to the world around us. In the search for more human engagement online, we neglect the people who closest and right next to us. The more time we spend on screen, the more profit social media companies can generate. The longer we stay on the platform, the more adverts can be served to us. The more adverts which are served to us, the more profit the company makes. We are trapped deep inside the 'growth hacking' model, which strives to ensure that growth is the only acceptable outcome for any social media company. More users online mean more adverts served means more advertising revenue. The revenues being generated by the giant social media companies is mind-boggling. Especially when compared to the low amount of taxation they are liable for. All beautifully choreographed to swim through the loopholes of corporation taxes which dance around legislation and morality like an Irish river-dancer on speed. It is within the social media corporations interest that we spend more time on their platforms. That we are greedy for more content. That we must keep scrolling, commenting, liking, sharing and most of all, posting the content so that others may gorge to try and satisfy their never-ending greed. The more we post, the longer we stay onsite. The longer we stay onsite, the more profit the company makes. Through the brands and corporations they represent, advertisers are just as responsible for our social media obesity and our greed for excessive screen time. Advertising agencies took their eye off the ball in the last two decades and allowed social media and technology companies to come to dominate the media landscape. In the past, the advertising and creative agencies were the gateway to mass media through marketing, be it on TV, Radio, Newspaper and or cinema, outdoor and even direct mailings. Without a creative media agency, you would find it very hard to even make a national campaign get noticed. Agencies demand high fees for creativity and planning as well as a cut of the media spend. Fast forward to today, creative and media agencies are subservient to Facebook and Google, which have become the only possible ways of reaching mass audiences through the online medium. Where more and more people spend their time online, social media and search channels held power. The sheer volume of the potential audience and the fact that they also gained in real-time valuable psychographic data as well as behavioural data even down to the point of checking out on a specific product or item. Attribution models would become apparent. If customer A clicks on banner B, they buy product C. The customer journey could be mapped and tracked. We could be influenced to buy based on our previous purchases or psychological insights into what makes us tick. This power of persuasion was the gold dust for social media corporations who had created the most powerful and profitable system of surveillance capitalism. And like any capitalist system, there is no end to its growth. Our data is not a finite resource. We leave endless streams of data exhaust behind us as we spend more and more of our waking (and sometimes even sleeping) hours online. We add more and more sensors and monitors into our homes and on our bodies. To complement or search and social data with our health data, the environmental data of our homes, how we use our smart rice cookers and what food we put inside of our smart fridges. The gyroscopes inside our phones track our every movement even when we are sitting still. Our smartwatches capture our heart rates and our blood oxygen levels as they count the number of steps we make and where exactly these steps take us. We willingly and often ignorantly freely provide our personal data to corporations. Who, in turn, sell our data to advertisers to feed their greed for profit. At some point, brands that know how to cash into the consciousness of people who care will start to become more privacy orientated. We can see this already with the likes of APPLE, who have made personal privacy one of the most forefront brand commitments in an apparent broadside towards Mark Zuckerberg and his Facebook Inc [1]. The internet tracking 'cookie' as we know it will change too as Google moves to dominate even more of the already well dominated personal

---

1 Apple's privacy battle with Facebook just became all-out war https://www.cnet.com/tech/services-and-software/apples-privacy-battle-with-facebook-just-became-all-out-war/

data arena. No more 'third party cookies' sounds so innocent yet, in reality, has been a terrifying history of web tracking ability by surveillance capitalism. The cycle of social media addiction is driven by greed. It is the greed of both the users and the dealers of technology. All are held together by the glue of marketing revenues. For our vices of GREED to succumb to the virtue of generosity, we must insist on a different use and path for our own personal data, so we, the users of technology, are not the sole source of the income for it. Brands and advertisers must also use the power of the marketing budgets for good. Rather than entrench consumers in the cycle of social media sin, they should use their profits to regain control of the media space and away from the technology giants. Will they be able to do this? I personally don't think so. As the technology giants now dictate through their networks' formats, the limits and benchmarks for creativity can be. Advertisers and creative agencies withdraw deeper into their shells. Self-congratulating each other and awarding each other with trophies and gongs. All for mediocre or cliched output, as they yearn for the yesteryears of Madmen when good copywriting and great creativity really did sell products as opposed to how big your pay per click media budget was. Social media technology companies should pay higher levels of taxation due to the harm they do to society to fund the future social media rehabilitation centres that will be required. Advertising agencies should be more careful with the brands they are paid to care for, grow and nurture. By feeding them to the social media giants, they have created a bastardised form of creative output and product branding, which only works if feed to the algorithm of greed. Our GREED will destroy us from within, and the greedy will always be hungry for more.

Social Media And The Seven Deadly Sins

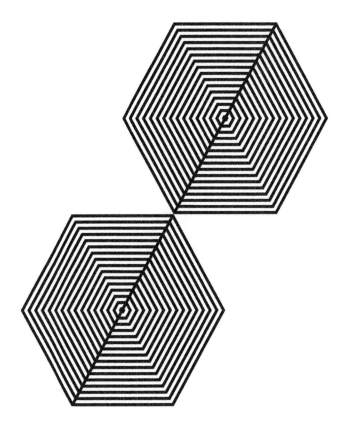

Chapter 8

Sloth

"Of all the cankers of human happiness, none corrodes it with so silent, yet so baneful, a tooth, as indolence."

— Thomas Jefferson

LAZY WITH THE TRUTH

WE BECAME LAZY. Subservient to mistruths. Facts should be sacred. Opinions should be free. Yet "the Earth is flat, and the global elite eats babies as a pizza topping"! Or so social media would have you believe.

We have instant access to all of humanities information at the push of a button. Yet, we seem to have no grasp of knowledge. Social media has fuelled and accelerated our age of stupidity, as portrayed in the 2006 sci-fi comedy 'Idiocracy'.

When you are browsing your Facebook, you can sometimes quickly feel like the character played by Luke Wilson in Idiocracy. It's easy to feel like the most intelligent person on the planet after 10 minutes on Facebook. People say some really dumb stuff on social media. And it's this spread of stupidity that has amplified the modern notion of fake news and modern conspiracy theories, all taking place in a global orgy of Chinese whispers with 4 billion participants. As Colonel Nathan R. Jessup testifies in The Few Good Men. The truth? You can't hand the truth!

High school wasn't the most comfortable place for me as a teenager. I guess that is the same story for us all. It can be a harsh and challenging environment in a battle with your peers and yourself as you develop from a child into a teenager and then into an adult. Rumours spread quickly in school, and the cruelty inherent in children within a school environment can lead to verbal bullying based on hearsay and mistruths. Yet, it was in high school, I learned such a valuable insight into what it means to understand the truth. I was lucky to have a really great teacher for history and sociology lessons. Mr Demby was a recently graduated teacher, which made a refreshing change from the dinosaurs who taught our other lessons. Mr Demby wasn't an "old school" type teacher who hadn't practised under the British school regimes of corporal punishment. Some of our teachers had neglected to recognise the 1989 Childen's Act (it wasn't ok to hurt kids anymore) and still bullied, beat and psychically assaulted their students as if it was a standard way to teach children their religious education studies. Not our Mr Demby; he had a new world approach to teaching. He was more like your mate than your teacher. It really worked. We trusted him and his lessons were always engaging and fun and full of two debates and conversation.

Mr Demby taught us some basic rules about analysing facts. In the context of history, we would look at different types of evidence and evaluate their validity. It was broken down into the following parts, Primary evidence and Secondary evidence. Primary sources refer to first-hand accounts by people who experienced the event. It can be a person's account of own feelings, actions, or experiences. Objects or documents that come directly from the person, place, or event being researched. Secondary sources are accounts by people who did not experience the event. These include a person's interpretation of someone else's feelings, actions, or experiences. Objects or documents that originate much later than the person, place, or event being researched. They often contain interpretations, analyses and synthesis of an event or series of events. Context is everything, and there is a difference between the content and the format and medium in which the context is being presented. Primary and secondary always relate to the content and never the format. At 15 years old, I could totally get my head around this concept. I was able to sophistically identify from historical records primary and secondary evidence and arrange and evaluate it accordingly. I often wonder how schoolchildren can understand such fundamental concepts of evidence validity when it seems so many adults can't? How have conspiracy theories been able to transcend all cultures and nations through the format of social media? To what extent are they being used as leverage in the new cold war of the disinformation age?

What makes your Mum start sharing posts about how 5G radiation causes COVID-19? What inspires your Brother to start sharing videos about Bill Gates desires to microchip and control every living person on the planet? How have we got here, and what can we do to try and ensure that we don't slip into a state of mass confusion? If we don't get out of this state, we will find that the truth is buried so deep within misinformation that it will become impossible to identify the primary and secondary sources ever again.

"If it can be destroyed by the truth, it deserves to be destroyed by the truth." — Carl Sagan

We all lie. Our social media is a testament to that. Even if you genuinely believe you are the most honest person in the universe, your social media is still lying on your behalf. There are white lies and not so white lies. Social media is a mirror of the self we want to be. Or at least the self we want others to see. Yet, our actions and behaviours on social media platforms allow administrators and data scientists to understand our subconscious and psyche far more than we ever can. For example, Facebook knows when you will break up with your partner many months before it actually happens[1]. Your actions and behaviours on the platform send strong signals through the network graph as your edge weight within your nodal network gets stronger and weaker between different friends and associates. This ability to primitively see your near future is one of the most fundamental reasons Facebook has become so profitable. They can literally predict your future based on the actions you perform on their site daily. The more time you spend on the platform, the deeper into your future, they can see. Unlike a fairground mystic, Facebook doesn't just want their palm crossed with two pieces of silver.

---

1 Facebook Knows When You Fall In Love, And That's Pretty Creepy https://www.forbes.com/sites/ianmorris/2016/12/31/facebook-knows-when-you-fall-in-love-and-thats-pretty-creepy/

They want to keep you engaged and onsite for as long as possible to extract as much potential advertising revenue as they can at the detriment of your health and wellbeing.

Take a look at your own social media. Is your Instagram feed just an endless stream of selfies? Do you post about things you have, something you want? If your posts are all about yourself, then you are locked within the black mirror of your phone. Your social media is for you and you only. You are creating an image of yourself that you want people to believe you are. You are not showing your true self. We all wear masks in everyday life. It is a defence mechanism and a way of protecting our inner feelings, thoughts and desires away from threat actors who may wish to use this against us. Yet on social media, we wear an even bigger mask; we behave like peacocks showing off glorious feathers in such a digital date with ourselves. We want to share our achievements, our proud moments of life, a new baby, a new job, a new home, a new car. We want to send birthday wishes and celebrate anniversary moments with our friends and family. We want to share the photos from our birthday party night out and that special Christmas day dinner with family.

I am old enough to remember what a real photo album looked like. My father is a photographer, and throughout the 70s and 80s, he made hundreds if not thousands of photos of our family. My mother being a teacher, meticulously organised the photos into albums and added handwritten captions and dates to all of the images. This meant later on in life, we could all sit around the table and open up a photo album and look back at the memories and special moments from our life. This tradition in the digital and social age has shifted. It is lost and gone. Replaced by the daily "memory" reminder in the form of a Facebook post or a time-capsule notification which replay back to us older images and posts we made on the platform many years ago.

If we are not careful, our memories will only exist on social media. Our collective consciousness will be owned by technology. In decades to come, we will forget the reality and only have memories that exist in this social media virtual reality. Our images, videos, words and thoughts will all be stored in vast data centres, which can at any moment be hacked, corrupted or destroyed at the flick of a switch or the blast of a solar storm. To preserve the truth and the historical record, we must retain analogue history alongside digital history. As well as publishing this book as an eBook, I will also print it as a paperback. At least as it to try and preserve it in some way for future generations. You must think about your memories and truth in this way. Don't allow social media companies to be the ones who own your memories. Don't allow the abuse of these memories to keep you on their platforms for longer and without you realising they are using your memories to hold you onsite longer. Without ownership of memories, it is hard to define the truth of the past. Without this, we can easily forget and be manipulated into becoming

SLOTHFUL with the truth. It will all be lost like tears in the rain.

* * * * *

FAKE NEWS READ ALL ABOUT IT

ALL THE SOCIAL media born conspiracies have in common and coincide with the concept of fake news. Social media has been the most influential and amplifying component of fake news as we know it. Fake news, in itself, is not a new concept. Adolf Hitler, for unknown reasons, altered a 1937 photograph to remove Minister of Propaganda Joseph Goebbels from the group shot. Benito Mussolini had a photo changed where he was horseback holding a sword aloft. He had the person holding his horse by the reins removed to make it look like he was in total control of the stallion. Chairman Mao was another photoshopper of his time, not shy to cut and paste an image he disagreed with. After he fell out with Po Ku, he altered images so the two would not be seen together. Even comrade Vladimir Lenin wasn't shy of a revolutionary cut and paste job. He had pictures of himself and Trotsky edited after denouncing him as a "scoundrel". Ever since the invention of the camera obscura, there has been a way to alter and edit photography because seeing is often seen as believing.

We looked in the previous chapter of GREED the concept around modern social media influencers. We looked at Edward Bernays and his ground-breaking book Propaganda, which still guides contemporary Public Relations and Advertising thinking today. Edward Bernays was a master of turning FAKE NEWS into REAL NEWS. What I coined many years ago is something called a MEDIA VIRUS. A stunt, a performance art, an event, an article or even just a piece of creative work could become a global news item and be reported on by all the primary news sources. For Edward Bernays is was precisely this. What would start as a well-orchestrated publicity stunt would become mainstream and headline news? On Sunday 31st of March 1929, Edward Bernays organised a large group of women to walk in the Easter Sunday Parade in New York. As they walked alongside the parade, they would be smoking cigarettes. Edward Bernays had coined the copy TORCHES OF FREEDOM for a campaign for his tabacco producing client. Their goal was to sell more cigarettes to women, who then were seen as unfeminine if they smoked. Edward Bernay's did associate smoking with the suffragette movement to suggest that it was a basic human right for women to smoke in public. As hundreds of women marched through the city of New York on that Easter Sunday in 1929, the news cameras rolled, and the paparazzi's flashed their strobes. The sight of so many women marching in unison, dressed in the Suffragette style, all happily smoking cigarettes was enough to cause a global media frenzy. Needless to say, from this day forward, it became socially acceptable for women to smoke in public and for Edward Bernays to double the sale of cigarettes for his client. Bernays had created a FAKE NEWS event. The women weren't marching for their rights. They were marching for the profit of capitalism. How many millions of smoking women would they go on to die from smoking-related diseases? FAKE NEWS always has a human cost.

For as long as there has been "news", there has been "fake news". What is new is how misinformation has to spread among huge audiences and on an international level. We are in the information age where technology allows us to send and receive data in milliseconds. We have the entire volume of human information at our fingertips, yet we seem to lack knowledge. The more information we have access to, the less understanding we seem to show. We have become lazy. Lazy with the truth. Our slothfulness rises to the top as we constantly face option paralysis. Too many choices, too much information. How do we process what is real and what is fake? We draw the line between satirical content and content that has a darker agenda and is pushed by hostile threat actors and or rogue nation-states seeking to destabilise democracy as we know it. Can the great firewalls of the east and the government control of internet services ensure information is not free? That net neutrality will remain a great ideal that was never achieved. Cyberspace is not a free space but an arm of government and a tool for authoritarian control? Fake news isn't just about manipulating elections and meddling in psychological warfare operations. Fake news is the bread and butter part of the public relations and advertising industries playbook. Social media has allowed PR companies to create grassroots communities to help them benefit their clients by creating organic-looking campaigns, protests, and community actions. Advertising agencies were able to harness the power of fake news to seed branded content into groups and communities by making it look and feel as if it was users generated and genuine content from adoring brand loyalists and so-called influencers.

In many ways, much of what we see on social media we presume it to be fake. Whether it is accurate or fake doesn't matter anymore. What matters is the share-ability and like-ability of the content. As fake news tends to be clickbait, controversial and polarising in nature, it succeeds to dominate the timelines by manipulation of the social media algorithm. Content that is engaging and keeping viewers on the platform is gaining higher traction as the longer a user stays on the platform the more adverts can be served to them, and the more revenue can be generated from that session. All social media works the same way. There is not a model of social media which isn't capitalising from surveillance capitalism and monetises your personal data in return for selling it to advertisers on behalf of brands and corporations.

* * * * * *

LOOSE CHANGE AND THE POST 9/11 WORLD

TWENTY YEARS SINCE the 9/11 attacks on the World Trade Towers, social media has come a long way. Two decades before the likes of Q-Anon and Flat-earthers were being mentioned on the prime time news and in the tabloid newspapers, conspiracy theories had found a new medium to take root and be seen by mass audiences. It's hard to imagine now, but just twenty years ago, the live images from the mainstream media as the exclusive channels to report in real-time to the world the events happening on the ground. Can you imagine what would happen if an event like this would happen today? Twitter would most likely meltdown. How many images and videos from first-person sources would be simultaneously uploaded to multiple social media channels in real-time at the same time. How many hundreds if not thousands of live streams would have been broadcast? There was no live streaming on social media back in 2001; it allowed for a certain amount of lag and time to pass before we started to see user-generated content from around the 9/11 event. The many thousands of witnesses and bystanders who filmed, photographed and captured the moments before, during and after the attack needed time to prepare their content, in some cases even get it developed and then digitised and transferred and uploaded to the internet or many submitting their footage to local and national TV stations as a means of getting it seen by a wider audience.

A crucial moment in this timeline comes four years after the September 11 attacks in 2005 and the online release of the documentary called Loose Change. Facebook was only a year old and a niche website for college students. It wasn't a mainstream social network and not available to the public; it was a closed network for American university students. It's hard to imagine now that there was no mainstream social media as we knew it today back in 2001. Social media at that time was in the form of ICQ chat rooms, message boards and forums. Social media was happening in the comment sections of blog sites and link aggregators like FARK and the Stile Project. Yet, there was one significant site that launched in 2005. Google Video. Google Video was a free video hosting service from Google, similar to YouTube, allowing video clips to be hosted on Google servers and embedded on other websites. The service was launched on January 25, 2005. A year later, YouTube was acquired by Google, and Google Videos began its evolution into its current form as a video search engine. And this is how people in 2005 got to hear about the film Loose Change.

There was no big theatrical release for the first cut of Loose Change. It was a film of its time, published for free online. Loose Change was created by Dylan Avery and put together on his laptop for a budget of just $2,000. What caught the audiences' attention was not only the narrative of the film but the thumping soundtrack, slick graphics with an authoritative voice-over with an internet style of scene editing. It was to set the benchmark of how future films around conspiracy topics should be done. The project started not as a documentary but as a screenplay in May 2003. Dylan Avery was researching an idea for a fictional script based on the 9/11 attacks. As Dylan researched more, he started to feel that there was enough evidence to support the many 9/11 conspiracy theories. He believed that the attacks were orchestrated by members of the United States government and started working on a non-fiction version of his screenplay, which would become Loose Change. The film, which started as a short 30-minute "internet film" went on to be viewed by millions of people and became one of the pillars of what would become known as the 9/11 Truth Movement. Dylan and his producers Korey Rowe, Jason Bermas, and Matthew Brown achieved this creating a film that made layers upon layers of analysis that would lead the viewer to the ultimate conclusion that Osama Bin Laden and al-Qaeda had nothing to do with the 9/11 attacks, regardless of the fact that in 1993 World Trade Centre had already been targeted by Islamic extremists and those attackers had received financing from al-Qaeda member Khalid Shaikh Mohammed, someone who would later admit to planning the 9/11 attacks. For Dylan and his team, this was irrelevant. Despite the great pain and anguish his conspiracy theories would cause to the families of the victims of 9/11 his film went on to be viewed by so many people that a third of all Americans believe that either the official version of events never happened, or that US officials knew the attacks were imminent, but did nothing to stop them[1]. Loose Change had gained a lot of celebrity backing from the Conspiracy influencers with the likes of radio host Alex Jones, Rosie O'Donnell and Charlie Sheen [2]. Loose Change had gone from a bedroom movie made on a cheap laptop to an internally viewed documentary that fuelled and sparked a mass movement of people based on proven factual errors and outright conspiracies. It also made a lot of money for the twenty-something-year-old men who created it. There is big business in conspiracy theories. Something the likes of Alex Jones knows all too well. Loose Change has set the stage and created the benchmark for all future conspiracy theories. The film went on to have many different cuts and variations, with a theatrical release on September 9, 2009, at the 9/11 Film Festival at the Grand Lake Theatre in Oakland, California. It was later published in DVD format going from the first 30-minute version produced for $2,000 to the final cut 70 min version made for $200,000. This is how you do conspiracy at scale.

In 2004, another documentary was produced and released, which offers a far more detailed and accurate view of Neo-Conservatism and Islamic terrorism. I would advise all of my readers to watch. If you view the 9/11 incident through the lens of this film, you will come to some rather sobering conclusions

1 'They're all forced to listen to us' https://www.theguardian.com/media/2007/jan/26/digitalmedia
2 Hollywoods 9/11 Idiot Brigade https://web.archive.org/web/20120112135332/http://www.nypost.com/p/pagesix/item_YIXNBlp6gXCY7Jzldwd7jJ%3Bjsessionid%3D1ED6372CC2FED0FCFAFB-10517F2786A9

that both the neoconservatives and Islamic extremists have a lot more in common than they do indifference. "The Power of Nightmares by British film maker Adam Curtis compares the rise of the neoconservative movement in the United States and the radical Islamist movement, drawing comparisons between their origins, and remarking on similarities between the two groups. More controversially, it argues that radical Islamism as a massive, sinister organisation, specifically in the form of al-Qaeda, is a myth, or noble lie, perpetuated by leaders of many countries—and particularly neoconservatives in the U.S.—in a renewed attempt to unite and inspire their people after the ultimate failure of utopian ideas. The Power of Nightmares was praised by film critics in Britain and the United States. Its message and content have also been the subject of various critiques and criticisms from conservatives and progressives [3]."

So while LOOSE CHANGE can easily be debunked on many levels and the inaccuracies laid bare, the tone of the movie and the sentiment of the film-makers was to lay down the feelings of mistrust in their governments that over half of the population of the USA feels. While Adam Curtis went on to deep dive into 9/11 and the ideological similarities and battles between Islamic Terrorism and Neo-Conservatism, it is still an outsider film of cult status. Whereas LOSE CHANGE can still be remembered as the mainstream outsider documentary of the century. There are still so many unanswered questions about 9/11, and still, so

3 The Power of Nightmares https://en.wikipedia.org/wiki/The_Power_of_Nightmares

many people feel and believe that the official explanation is not the reality. Hence we live in a world where the truth is constantly shapeshifting, and that has allowed Social Media to become the primary medium of choice for sowing the seeds of mass confusion.

* * * * * *

THE Q CONSPIRACY

HOW DO YOU make the jump from what can only be described as the arse end of the internet to become social media mainstream to infiltrate the minds of hundreds of millions of people. With the full support of the Commander and Chief, the president of the United States of America. To become the buzzword of international media whilst simultaneously being described as domestic terrorists [1]? QAnon knows how.

The Q conspiracy often referred to as QAnon, or simply Q, believes that a cabal of satanic paedophiles run an international child sex trafficking ring. The cabal is made up of the worlds powerful elite, including politicians, financiers and celebrities. While there are cases to illustrate that such international child sex trafficking rings are operating, the serious allegations against the now-deceased Jeffrey Epstein only strengthen the Q conspiracy in its ability to recruit new members, it is utterly unproven and false to suggest that such a cabal exists and to conspire specifically against Donald Trump during his term in office. This is what the Q Conspiracy had morphed into by the time we had reached the 2020 presidential election in the USA.

So, where did it begin? In terms of conspiracy theories, the Q Conspiracy is a modern phenomenon created within social media, starting on the fridges of it. We can trace the origins back

1 Quantifying The Q Conspiracy: A Data-Driven Approach to Understanding the Threat Posed by QAnon https://thesoufancenter.org/wp-content/uploads/2021/04/TSC-White-Paper_QA-non_16April2021-final-1.pdf

to the /pol/ board of the 4Chan forum when on October 28th 2017, a user named "Q Clearance Patriot" posted a thread titled "Calm Before the Storm". So what is 4Chan? 4Chan is an English language "imageboard" (which means an image-based message board). It allows its users to anonymously post on various topics ranging from anime and manga to video games, music, literature, fitness, politics, and sports, among others. While this may seem quite random and varied, and its no design no thrills style may seem unappealing, the website 4chan receives more than 20 million unique monthly visitors, with more than 900,000 posts made daily [2]. 4Chan was created by Christopher Poole, a self-proclaimed "American Internet entrepreneur" Poole was voted the world's most influential person of 2008 in the Time100 list. The voting was compromised, and there were claims of ballot stuffing through automated voting programs. It's doubtful Poole was as influential as the vote results suggested. However, his creation of 4Chan would be 2020 become a powerful medium for amplifying global conspiracy theories that would lead thousands of people to march on and create an insurrection at the US Capitol building. Poole was 4Chan's administrator for more than 11 years before stepping down in January 2015.

Interestingly he then went on to work at Google from 2016 to 2021. I wonder why he quit? Or was he fired? Google likes to recruit the "bad boys" of technology. Don't be evil, hey say. By September of 2015, it was announced that a "Japanese internet

2 4chan advertising rates and statistics https://www.4chan.org/advertise

entrepreneur", Hiroyuki Nishimura, founder of the Japanese BBS 2channel, would take over as the site's owner, and he remains as the administrator to this day. Within the 4Chan site, there can be found a lot of conspiratorial content and blatant antisemitism and racism. There is plenty of misogyny and sexism too, with an unhealthy obsession with hardcore pornography and even child pornography [3]. Its become a place known for cyberbullying [4] and a medium for leaking personal and sensitive information hacked from unsuspecting people and especially celebrities [5]. 4Chan represents the very heart of what we would call "Internet culture". It has been a place that generated many MEME's as well as amplifying and propagating existing MEME's. Its anonymous posting style and no registration policy allows an audience of mostly young American men between the ages of 18-34 [6] to post crap and waste time whilst they should be studying for their college. It helps them feel become part of a techno counter-culture within an obscure part of the expansive and infinite cyberspace. Needless to say, this fertile breeding ground of disenfranchised young men was the perfect springboard for the Q Conspiracy to seed and blossom. Yet it seems like quite a jump to go from men posting Anime porn on anonymous message boards to your Grandma sharing #SaveTheChildren or

3 Another 4chan User Gets Busted By FBI http://www.thesmokinggun.com/documents/internet/another-4chan-user-gets-busted-fbi
4 Face Behind The Name: Meet Matthew Riskin Bean, Convicted 4chan Cyberstalker http://www.thesmokinggun.com/buster/4chan/face-behind-name-meet-matthew-riskin-bean-convicted-4chan-cyberstalker
5 Apple confirms accounts compromised but denies security breach https://www.bbc.com/news/technology-29039294
6 Advertising statistics 4Chan https://www.4chan.org/advertise

#PizzaGate on her Facebook. Yet this is precisely what happened.

In the run-up to the 2020 presidential elections in the USA, I remember observing stalls popping up all over America selling t-shirts and apparel in support of President Trump. It seemed that one of the best-selling t-shirts had a large "Q" overlaid on top of an American flag. At Trump rallies, you could clearly see people wearing t-shirts and holding up placards that had the statements "WE ARE Q" and the abbreviated "WWG1WGA" meaning "where we go one, we go all". Everyone it seemed in the Trump camp was ready for "THE STORM" and in full support of a conspiracy created in an obscure message board just three years prior. This, of course, isn't usual, and it can only be because of some serious amplification by organised actors. Of all the conspiracy theories on all the image boards, how and why did the Q Conspiracy become a national concern and an international movement of people. Social media is how and our inherent vice of SLOTH leading us to become lazy with the truth. From a branding perspective, the Q Conspiracy is impressive. To make the jump from an internet MEME to a globally recognised brand of a movement in just three years is something many companies try and fail to achieve using even the very best advertising agencies in the world. It would seem even more apparent that Q had a little help from his friends, who in turn are not so friendly to the United States of America.

The Soufan Center is an independent non-profit centre

offering research, analysis, and strategic dialogue on global security challenges and foreign policy issues. They analysed 166,820 Q-Anon categorised Facebook posts between January 2020 and February 2021. They identified that the level of foreign influence within the Q-Anon posts was constant throughout the year at an average of 19% of all the posts analysed. However, they did identify notable peaks correlating with events in the United States, such as the domestic outbreak of COVID-19 and the 2020 presidential election. Russia is considered the most capable and sophisticated driver of disinformation and was identified as the main amplifier of Q-Anon posts, with 44% of the posts stemming from Russian administrators. Yet this was closely followed by content originating from China with 42% of the post volume. By the end of the 2020 election, China had become the most active state actor amplifying Q-Anon conspiracy theories. China's actions, unlike Russia, were less likely to be aimed at influencing the US elections but more related to the ongoing tensions arising from COVID-19 and the build-up of military power in the pacific region, as well as the continuous attention being brought on them when it comes to alleged human rights abuses.

A recent report from the Office of the Director of National Intelligence (ODNI) concludes that China "did not deploy interference efforts and considered but did not deploy influence efforts intended to change the outcome of the US Presidential election." However, according to our data, by September 2020,

China had surpassed Russia as the primary origin of Foreign Influence online within QAnon narratives specifically. This trend line has continued in 2021. From January 1 to February 28, 2021, 58% of posts came from administrators in China— at more than double the rate of those from Russian administrators. China's goal, most likely, is to sow further discord and division among the American population [7].

The aim of amplifying conspiracy theories from the point of view of state actors is to undermined authority in the target nation. The cold war may have ended back in the 1990s, but the hot psychological warfare never stopped. The battle of ideology moved from the battle of left and right, communism versus capitalism, to a struggle between corporate oligarchy versus gangster oligarchy, all united the same unifying ideology and methodology of surveillance capitalism. Social media has allowed subversion and psychological warfare in every home and every pocket of every person connected to the internet and social media. No longer are pamphlets dropped from an Aeroplane into the hostile territory, but a MEME style post is organically pushed down your timeline and facilitated by the algorithms created by the tech corporations who claim to have your best interests at heart. If the content keeps you engaged, they don't really care if the content is harmful, misleading and amplified by hostile actors. If the content keeps you on the platform and engaging,

---

7 Quantifying The Q Conspiracy: A Data-Driven Approach to Understanding the Threat Posed by QAnon https://thesoufancenter.org/wp-content/uploads/2021/04/TSC-White-Paper_QA-non_16April2021-final-1.pdf

it's making their profit, and the algorithm will give the content high priority to be seen by even more people just like you. Where this content succeeds is how we use social media.

We have become lazy with the truth and custom to clickbait headlines, reacting to things without understanding the full context or even the source of the information we are reading and engaging with. We allow our cognitive biases to take control and the primary most fundamental biases of social proof to under rule our ability to analyse content to decide its validity. When we see so many of our friends have already liked and shared a piece of content, we validate it as something that we should share and like. And this is precisely how conspiracies such as Q-Anon multiply to the point where families start to be torn apart. The aim of hostile actors and nation-states is to create chaos amongst their competitors to assert leverage where military confrontation would not be an advantage. By destabilising societies through sowing discord, confusion and distrust, populations can be shaken into a state of mass confusion, unable to see the constant shapeshifting of the truth around them. They will become less likely to believe in their political leaders and less likely to be law-abiding citizens.

* * * * * *

THE EARTH IS FLAT

IF I WAS to tell you that the Earth was flat, what would you say? How could you convince me that the Earth was, in fact, spherical? Or at best, a potato-shaped lump of rock spinning around on an axis of 23.5 degrees rotating at 67,000 miles per hour on a 365-day orbit 584,000,000 miles around the star we call the sun! Maybe that was already too many facts for you to respond to? It could be argued that many observable things clearly illustrate that the Earth is, in fact not flat. Weather patterns and systems being one good example. The best is one of the many thousands of satellite images or photography from the International Space Station or many American, Russian, Chinese, and human-crewed space missions that put humans into low earth orbit. If you are old and once rich enough, you might have even flown at supersonic speed on Concorde. Or been a fighter/bomber pilot and flown at high altitude. All of these experiences will have shown you the upper atmosphere and the ability to see the curvature of the Earth. Yet still, the theory of a flat Earth can be traced way back in human mythology to early Egypt and Mesopotamian thought, whose myths state the world was portrayed as a disk floating in the ocean. By the early 4th century BC Plato wrote about a spherical Earth, and by about 330 BC, his former student, Aristotle, had provided strong empirical evidence for this. Yet, that wasn't going to be the end of that story. The flat earth conspiracy would survive thousands of years into the 21st century, where thanks to social media, it once again became a popular idea. No, Terry Pratchett (bless his soul) and his Discworld are not to blame for this. If you believe the Earth is flat, then you think that every pilot and captain of every ship that has ever flown or sailed from point A to point B is part of this grand conspiracy. You would think that it is an almost possible task to stop anyone of these professional navigators from spilling the beans. Why hasn't any captain of any ship ever reported a sighting of the great ice wall? Simply because it doesn't exist.

To me, the flat Earth conspiracy seems totally barmy. How anyone can find themselves believing such a blatant and obvious falsehood, I will never understand. Yet, I will try to understand this for the sake of the book. It is down to our slothfulness. It can be hard work to make friends. Especially if you are more of an introverted type. Groups and situations can be daunting and often quite unappealing and somewhat intimidating to fit into real-world communities. Yet online, you can be whoever you want to be. On social media, you can easily choose to create yourself of how you wish others to see you. Wear a mask and become the superhero you always wanted to be without fear of being ridiculed in real-life situations. When you look at the leading players behind the flat Earth conspiracy theory, you will start to discover a definite pattern in the type of people who promote it.

An example of the type of character (and I call him a

character on purpose as he is playing a role in a narrative that's only outcome is to benefit the players in the game) is Mark Sargent. His Wikipedia entry [1] states "Mark K. Sargent is one of the leading proponents of, and recruiters for, the flat Earth conspiracy theory in the United States. According to critics, his YouTube videos have greatly accelerated the popularisation of modern flat Earth belief, one without scientific merit."

Mark has made a name for himself and becomes somewhat a fringe celebrity within the flat world of flat-earthers. A single man with plenty of time on his hands enabled Mark to uncover the truth about our planet. His own words, not me being snide in attacking his single white, middle-aged male status. "Most people get married and have kids. But if you don't, you have a huge amount of free time on your hands." Mark Sargent said in a 2019 interview with Andrea Brown of the Washington Herald Net [2].

Social media has helped Mark find his place in a community as a thought leader and figurehead. Social media has transformed him into a shy and lonely individual into someone who is invited to be a guest speaker in front of thousands of like-minded people. It has enabled him to sell t-shirts and create ad revenue from video content and drive hundreds of thousands of people through web pages knowing that each click has a dollar value assigned to it. Social media conspiracy is an industry. Not just a financial one,

1 Mark Sargent (flat Earth proponent) https://en.wikipedia.org/wiki/Mark_Sargent_(flat_Earth_pro-ponent
2 He's semi-famous for being flat-out wrong about Earth https://www.heraldnet.com/news/hes-semi-famous-for-being-flat-out-wrong-about-earth/

but an initiative of networking and connections. Of friendships, alliances, as well as an industry of rivalry, competitiveness and infighting. Within an online community, be it flat-earthers, Q-Anon or whoever it may be, you will find these elements.

In many cases, the original concept of why all these people are gathered together becomes almost irrelevant. They are united in some shared beliefs no matter how far fetched, and farcical they may seem. What holds them together is their sense of community and friendship and their own ego's and ambitions to become the next Alex Jones or Mark Sargent. To lead the sheep out of the penned in fields and out into the open valleys whilst parting any oceans which lay in the way of their epic voyage to their self proclaimed Eldorado of truth. An Eldorado that they never find.

The Earth is not flat. No one has ever, to this date, posted a photograph of the so-called ice wall. I wonder why Mark Sargent hasn't yet chartered his own ship and sailed out to the edge of the Earth to prove us all wrong? Surely he can afford it by now.

* * * * * *

COVIDIOTS

I STARTED WRITING this book as the world was entering the first unknown stages of what would soon become a global pandemic. COVID-19 is a highly infectious disease that, by now, we are all very familiar with. I don't intend to start writing about the coronavirus in great detail, but it should be noted that it was not only an infectious disease that was dangerous to our health. It was also a viral concept that infected our minds and our ability to determine fact from fiction thanks to our decade-long slothfulness with the truth through our abuse of social media. Conspiracy theories and fake news spread faster than the actual virus. While we all learned about reproduction rates and the "R" number (when the value of R is greater than 1 the disease starts to spread uncontrollably) it got me wondering if we needed such a "R" rating for social media content and the vast volume of conspiratorial and false information that infected so many people at such high speeds. COVID conspiracies have cumulated in mass protests happening all around the world. Anti-Vaxers, Anti-Maskers and Anti-lockdown protests have become a regular thing the longer the pandemic raged for. The general theory behind the demonstrations is that COVID-19 is a conspiracy by the global elite or shadow governments, AKA deep state, to control the general population.

The vaccination jab is a conspiracy lead by Bill Gates and

the new world order so that Microsoft can insert microchips inside each and every human being to track and control us. I ask myself how did conspiracies like this even get off the ground when we all carry multi-sensory audiovisual devices which can be tracked and monitored at all times in the form of our mobile phones. Logic doesn't play a role in conspiracies theories. Not to mention that Microsoft makes software, not hardware chips. Bill Gates and his wife Melinda have done more to help people around the world get vaccinated against diseases like Malaria that I find it so ignorant and foolish of people to believe in and share content and posts on their social media which claim Bill Gates wants to kill children through vaccination and that he wants to insert micro-ships inside your body. Yet here we are. It would seem that millions upon millions of people believe this. As they have "done their own research" through social media and alternative websites. They have watched the modern-day versions of what Loose Change once was. They have seen the videos. They know that the information war is against the "experts" and "scientists" who are all part of the new world order (a modern term for what really is outright antisemitism) and that we should all listen to the alternative voices from social media and online videos. Who would you rather trust? A qualified doctor or scientist over trusting someone making a blog and YouTube videos from their backroom behind a green screen and a $200 webcam. Of course, not all of the misinformation around COVID-19 is coming from "alternative amateur experts". There has been a huge effort by threat actors and operatives of nation-states to facilitate the spread of misinformation and disinformation concerning the COVID-19 pandemic. The aim of sowing distrust within governments and authority as a means of military and political leverage. Many of the players we have seen active in the Q-Conspiracy chapter are involved in the COVID-19 misinformation arena. And for a good reason. The more we are distracted and disorientated by conflicting and untruthful information, the longer we stay in our status of slothfulness. The lazier we become, the easier it is to guide our digital journeys down the path of clickbait links and sensationalised content, the more the social media algorithm will feed us. The radicalisation rabbit hole is what the algorithms have created. The more you click and engage with fake news, the deeper down the hole you will go entering a vast echo chamber of content that works towards entrenching your point of view no matter how detached from fact and reality it may have become.

During COVID-19, which is still ongoing at the time of writing this book, all of the major social media companies came under the spotlight as we soon saw that the spread of disinformation could be and was becoming as deadly as the actual COVID-19 virus itself. It had already been widely flagged that social media content feed algorithms were becoming responsible for the radicalisation of people on various fronts and for multiple causes, subjects and issues. YouTube, in particular, had been spotlighted many times in the view of how its recommended videos algorithm works and the impact of such an algorithm was having on people[1].

Facebook, Twitter, and YouTube/Google all decided to take some action to give the impression that they should be a force for truth in a time of a global medical emergency. This was obviously too little, too late, but the implications of their actions will change the balance of social media as we move forward. All the social media giants tried to flag misinformation and or attach disclaimers to users posts that mentioned COVID-19 related content. All of the social media services erred in doing so [2]. Valuable content which was either open to debate or even debunking COVID-19 conspiracies was flagged while at the same time disinformation was being allowed to circulate.

On May 11th 2020 Twitter published an article on heir blog titled "Updating our approach to misleading information" [3]. In this blog post they gave further guidance to their continuity strategy during COVID-19 [4] which they had published in March 2020. The top priority for Twitter was "keeping the service running and the Tweets flowing". As the pandemic worsened, Tweets increased.

1 COVID-RELATED MISINFORMATION ON YOUTUBE The Spread of Misinformation Videos on Social Media and the Effectiveness of Platform Policies https://demtech.oii.ox.ac.uk/wp-content/uploads/sites/93/2020/09/YouTube-misinfo-memo.pdf
2 Facebook, YouTube Erred in Censoring Covid-19 'Misinformation' https://www.bloomberg.com/opinion/articles/2021-06-07/facebook-youtube-erred-in-censoring-covid-19-misinformation
3 Updating our approach to misleading information https://blog.twitter.com/en_us/topics/product/2020/updating-our-approach-to-misleading-information
4 An update on our continuity strategy during COVID-19 https://blog.twitter.com/en_us/topics/company/2020/An-update-on-our-continuity-strategy-during-COVID-19

And with this increase in volume, Twitter needed to broaden their definition of harm in order "to address content that goes directly against guidance from authoritative sources of global and local public health information". Ultimately this would mean adding disclaimers to President Donald Trump's Tweets as well as disclaimers to many other's Tweets that contained information or statements that Twitter deemed went "directly against guidance from authoritative sources of global and local public health information". When you have an authoritative source of global information such as the President of the United States of America that maybe we should be drinking bleach, do you think a disclaimer on a tweet or even censoring and deleting a tweet is going to change much? It's probably already gone too far. Least we forget, for many, many years, Twitter had been supportive of Donald Trump's Twitter behaviour as his Tweetstorms and especially as president gave Twitter a lot of attention and prime time news coverage. Twitter had allowed Donald Trump to break their own community guidelines and policies on abusive behaviour for many years to enable Trump to taunt, bully, and make threats to individuals and entire nations. Yet somehow, during the global pandemic, they suddenly realised the error of their ways and decided now was the time that they started to be the good guy. Twitter is very inconsistent here and comes out of this looking very shallow. Even more so to the point where they and all the other social media sites, banned the president from their networks and deleted his accounts. This is something we will look at in more detail in the chapter PRIDE.

Trump said some stupid things during the peak of the COVID-19 pandemic. For all we know, the height of the pandemic is yet to happen. However, as mass vaccination programs roll out around the world, our only hope is to vaccinate enough people before a vicious variant like DELTA takes off and sets us all back to square one and in eternal lockdown. With our only protection, old t-shirts wrapped around our faces, and an endless list of home delivery apps for groceries and restaurant takeaways. As soon as I could get vaccinated, I did. I have had two jabs of the Moderna vaccine. I was disappointed that my 5G signal didn't get stronger. I still had to spell check this book manually as my Bill Gates microchip didn't allow me to automatically edit and spell check this book remotely through some internal share-point exchange. Bill, if you are tuning in and watching me type this, I am sorry that I have used a Macintosh since I was 8 years old. Maybe one day I will buy an Xbox, but I think it's doubtful. Don't hate me, bro.

COVID-19 Conspiracies have made me re-evaluate friendships and social media connections. As the lockdown went into full swing, I could see more and more of my "friends" and social media associates starting to share highly misleading content that was incredibly naive and only aiding in the spread of disinformation. At first, I tried to argue the toss with them. To deflect their posts and content with the facts. Yet the facts of the situation don't mean anything to people who have become so entrenched in conspiratorial views. "DO YOUR RESEARCH", they would respond in capital letters. Offering me links to non-clinical opinions of snake oil salesmen or alternative medicine healers. 5G IS KILLING TREES; MAN JUST LOOK HOW ITS SPREADING COVID.

Oh yeah, I would say. How does a radio wave do that? Psychics would tell you a radio wave can only slightly heat up the molecules that it passes through. Nothing more, nothing less. It is harmless. DO YOUR RESEARCH. They would respond with a link to a YouTube video showing examples of 5G antennas hidden inside street lamps (which, of course, they are not). It soon became apparent that was no hope for these so-called friends. They wouldn't listen to reason or logic, and they would get quite forceful in pushing links to blatant disinformation sites. They would also start to get quite nasty and name calling.

You are a shill if you disagree with their point of view. You are a sheep, and you can't think for yourself if you don't follow their sheep-like herd mentality. It's as if by having Google search, you are somehow more knowledgeable than a scientific expert with a specialism and doctorate in particle psychics. The idea that all the world experts are on the side of the evil child-eating lizard people and the people who make poorly designed blogs and YouTube videos with free Movie Maker software are the ones we should be listening to. I made the mistake of getting angry. I would start to argue with people who posted blatant conspiracy content that would appear on my timeline. I would belittle them and humiliate them in a massive response of post comment spam with logic, evidence, links, and valid points of reference. To the moment where I realise it wouldn't change their minds. So I just called them names and told them to go fuck themselves and deleted our social media connections online, and ended our friendships in reality. I realise now this probably wasn't the best way to handle it. If you want to try and turn someone's opinion around you, you have to be a little more subtle and a little more persuasive in a gentle manner. You catch more flies with honey than you do with vinegar. However, I am pleased that it made me re-evaluate who I want as social media friends. I cut down my friend's list by hundreds.

I had read somewhere that if you have more than 200 connections on your social media, it starts to become too much of an over-extended network. The chances and probability that you are closely connected to people above this 200 number begin to diminish. Sociologists will tell you that you are only five handshakes away from the next president of the United States of America. That is how closely connected human interactions and networks are. In the day and age of social media is probably only two to three nodes away on the social graph in the day and age. Well, let me be clear. I no longer want to shake hands with the next president of the United States of America because friend counts are a vanity metric. Sure, I probably know at least 500 people in this world. But do I need them all on a friends list to have their posts in my timeline every single day? No, I do not. Because honestly, I don't really care. And nor do you, you just haven't realised it yet. You are still in social media denial and not ready to admit it. You might get there one day.

The longer COVID-19 and the lockdown continue, the more time people spent online and more so on social media. The more bullshit that appeared on my timeline, the more people I deleted and unfollowed. It is not about creating an echo chamber where you only have opinions and views that you agree with, far from it. I like to have a very diverse and different timeline of content. I like to be challenged and have new ideas and points of view presented to me regularly and daily. And that is why I deleted COVDIOTS. Their rhetoric is so dull, predictable, illogical and downright uncreative. "The global elite want to keep you locked down at home". Do they? Surely they want to keep us at work and paying taxes, so the sovereign debt instalments get paid each month? Make up your minds? The COVIDIOTS just didn't have the MEME'ing ability of the likes of the REDDIT gaming community. And this is what makes their content so weak from a creative and social media point of view. COVIDITS make crap content. And this can be seen in the entirely illogical and mashed up grouping of people it has created.

When I saw Anti-Vaxer and Anti-Lockdown protestors

storm the Reichstag in Berlin, it was incredible to see standing side by side hippies and neo Nazis [5]. Both united in their COVIDIOT status. What has become of the so-called left and right when hippies can protest alongside neo Nazis. That is purely and only as a result of social media. We became lazy with the truth.

Social media companies Facebook, Twitter, LinkedIn and Google's YouTube, have taken action. They have started to close down the accounts of people who peddle disinformation. The chain reaction of high profile celebrities and politicians being banned from the platform has the knock-on effect of being banned from all platforms. The most notable de-platforming was of President Donald Trump. While this is unprecedented in history, having the voice of the most powerful man in the world turned off by certain sections of the 'media' DJT was not the first person to ban social media. There had been many before him, and there will be many after him. The "Alt-Right" and the "COVIDIOTS" have had to find a different outlet for their views. New social media sites and messaging services have appeared to cater for the echo chamber of conspiracy theorists where they can gather and discuss their views on Israeli cyber capabilities and how the term "global elite" is a modern day version of labelling Jews in the same way as the Nazi's dehumanised Jews by calling them rodents, vermin and insects. Walking through the streets of Prague, as I am sure can be seen in many cities in Europe, you will

---

5 Far-Right Germans Try to Storm Reichstag as Virus Protests Escalate https://www.nytimes.com/2020/08/31/world/europe/reichstag-germany-neonazi-coronavirus.html

see graffiti with statements like "COVID19 = JEWISH" and "BILL GATES = JEW". Considering that it is totally and widely accepted that COVID-19 was ordinated in Wuhan, China and that Bill Gates and his parents attended the United Church of Christ, it can be safe to say the Gates family are most definitely of Christian background and of Irish / English and German heritage. So no, Bill Gates is not Jewish, and COVID-19 is not a Jewish conspiracy to enslave the world.

The mere fact these concepts have spread from social media postings to graffiti in public places shows how dangerous our social media-induced slothfulness has become. As we slowly start to poke our heads outside of a lock-downed world, the sceptical and unvaccinated will be the ones that put everyone at risk. Unless we reach over the tipping point of the vaccinated population, there is always a chance that the virus or a mutated version of the virus will again take hold and reset the new normal back to the beginning. While I think it is totally acceptable and often somewhat wise to be sceptical of governments and try to hold power to account, we shouldn't allow our slothfulness to override our senses and subconsciousness, which is precisely what social media does to us daily if you heavily use social media.

Take a break from social media. It's made you become too lazy with the truth. Discover the real world outside of online content. Challenge your own narrative and deeply held prejudices. Break out of your own echo chamber.

"The truth may be puzzling. It may take some work to grapple with. It may be counterintuitive. It may contradict deeply held prejudices. It may not be consonant with what we desperately want to be true. But our preferences do not determine what's true." — Carl Sagan

Rory Wilmer

Social Media And The Seven Deadly Sins

Chapter 9

Wrath

—

"Fire! Fire! Fire! Fire! Now you've heard it, not shouted in a crowded theatre admittedly as I realize I seem now to have shouted it in the Hogwarts dining room but the point is made."

— Christopher Hitchens

"Freedom of speech is meaningless unless it means the freedom of the person who thinks differently"

— Rosa Luxemburg

FROM LIFESTREAM TO LIVESTREAM

As we became lazy with the truth, our slothfulness leads us to wrath. We became angry. Angry people click more. For the generations who have grown up in the era of reality TV and the likes of the Big Brother series, the Truman Show-style 24/7 reality of live camera feeds is nothing out of the ordinary. Big Brother was created and produced by a Dutch company called Endemol and was first launched onto our TV screens in 1999 and syndicated internationally. The concept was that a group of 'housemates' would enter a sealed house cloaked in hidden cameras.

The housemates wouldn't be able to leave the house until the moment at which the viewing public voted them out. Viewers would each week call a premium phone number and cast their vote for which member of the house they wanted to see evicted. This would continue until there was only one person left in the place who was crowned the winner. The Big Brother TV show is a result of an evolution of the internet and early social media. Specifically the creation of the 'web camera' and the beginning of 'lifecasting'.

Let us put to one side that, of course, the sex industry was one of the first pioneers in the digital space to advance technology, as with most of the internet and social media, pornographers were there first. Live sex shows and personal 1-on-1 strip shows by 'cam girls' were some of the first live streaming broadcasts to happen over the internet. However, the very first live stream from a webcam isn't as sexy as you might think. Unless you get excited by watching a hot steaming coffee pot. And that is not a metaphor. In 1990 Cambridge University Computer Science Department had their webcam pointed at a coffee machine in the Trojan Room. Initially, the camera feed ensured students who needed to be immediately caffeinated were not disappointed by turning up to an empty coffee pot. The web camera ensured that the post remained fully operational to serve at all times. What started as a feed on their internal network was broadcast live to the web and gained international notoriety as a symbol of the fledgling World Wide Web. Decades later, it would become social media live streaming. The coffee pot live stream was retired in 2001, more than a decade after it started to beam its first images. It had become front-page news and a symbol of the millennium we had just entered. There were other early precursors to live-streaming that happened before Big Brother hit the worlds TV sets. A group of friends living in a Manhattan apartment set up multiple web cameras in their loft apartment. They started streaming their everyday life in a limited time experiment called "You live with us" - at least, that is what I remember it being called. Still, I am struggling to find online references to it. I remember three people living in an apartment and a black and white image feed from various rooms in the house. The website also offered alongside the live camera feed a live chat feature. Viewers would write messages to the web-casters as well as start conversations between themselves. At the time, this was something totally new. It sounds perfectly normal as I write it today, like an everyday Twitch stream or a YouTube live video. In the 1990s, this was something totally new, and we had not seen before on the worldwide web.

Before there was social media live-streaming, there was something called life-streaming. Lifestreaming is an act of documenting and sharing aspects of one's daily social experiences online via a lifestream website that collects the things person chooses to publish (e.g. photos, tweets, videos) and presents them in reverse-chronological order. Lifestreaming content would be captured by the life streamer wearing a computer. The term "lifestream" was coined by Eric Freeman and David Gelernter at Yale University in the mid-1990s to describe "...a time-ordered stream of documents that functions as a diary of your electronic life; every document you create and every document other people send you is stored in your lifestream. The tail of your stream contains documents from the past (starting with your electronic birth certificate). Moving away from the tail and toward the present, your stream contains more recent documents—papers in progress or new electronic mail; other documents (pictures, correspondence, bills, movies, voice mail, software) are stored in between. Moving beyond the present and into the future, the stream contains documents you will need: reminders, calendar items, to-do lists. The point of lifestreams isn't to shift from one software structure to another but to shift the whole premise of computerized information: to stop building glorified file cabinets and start building (simplified, abstract) artificial minds; and to store our electronic lives inside [1]." Lifestreaming was seen as the equivalent to an artists sketchbook. "I like to think of a lifestreaming as today's digital equivalent of Leonardo da Vinci's notebooks [...] da Vinci 's recorded notes, drawing, questions and more in his notebooks. Some of these were quite mundane (grocery lists and doodles), others were not. But their body of work was overtime, a view of a one individual's mind [2]."

Lifestreaming was happening as early as the late 1980s. Some of the first wearable computers and radio antennas created clumsy-looking and awkward cyborg-like costumes for the lifestreamers. As the technology advanced, wearable computer technology got smarter and smaller. To the point, today where we can have a mobile phone in our pocket and wearable google glasses style cameras and head-mounted GoPro's. With "follow me" drones that can capture our every move and broadcast them live and real-time on the internet and to our social media networks. Yet rather than becoming a way to document our lives for creative thought and prosperity. The Livestream became a portal for our WRATH to be broadcast to the world and to inspire

1 Welcome to the Yale Lifestreams homepage! http://cs-www.cs.yale.edu/homes/freeman/lifestreams.html
2 Steve Rubel. "Why Lifestream? To model Leonardo da Vinci diaries" https://web.archive.org/web/20130528005738/http://www.steverubel.com/why-lifestream-to-model-leonardo-da-vinci

racial bullying to incite mass murder. To distribute real-time snuff videos and even showcase the rape and sexual abuse of minors. Are you serious? Yes I am as the next section will show us. One man a lifestream / livestream can have brutal and deadly consequences.

CHIRSTCHURCH

Friday, March 15th 2019, started just like any other day in Aukland, New Zealand. People were looking forward to the autumn weekend ahead and making most of the weather before the winter season. Yet it wasn't just any Friday for Australian white supremacist Brenton Tarrant. Brenton had put into motion a plot to murder as many innocent Muslim men as he could with the intention of live-streaming the entire event to Facebook and the world. It should be of no surprise that Tarrant's social media activities can be traced back to the 4Chan forum, where he is said to have started being an active part of the community from the age of 14 [3]. While much is written about Tarrant and his early life and childhood leading up to his mass shooting event, I don't need to go deeper into these details here and now. There is much in-depth analysis of this white supremacist mass murderer online and in print. What is essential to look at here in the content of this book and this chapter of wrath is how his live streaming of

3 Report finds lapses ahead of New Zealand mosque attack https://web.archive.org/web/20201208200943/https://apnews.com/article/intelligence-agencies-shootings-brenton-tarrant-new-zealand-new-zealand-mosque-attacks-d8217fa30fe4eeba45fb001b77857385

the massacre in real-time would have enormous implications for Facebook, the ethics of social media algorithms and the overall concepts of live streaming as a medium. Before Tarrant's attack, which killed 51 people and injured 40 more, were all the social media signals that Tarrant was about to commit such an atrocity. His social media and YouTube postings showed clearly that his network graph and edge rank behaviour was closely aligned with far ideology and white supremacy. Tarrant had started to clarify his views and, moreover, what his intention was. Yet the social media algorithms didn't see this as a warning; they saw it as a signal to serve him yet more radical content to entrench and confirm his views. Tarrant's wrath was being amplified by social media. Not only by other people who shared his twisted and racist views but by the very medium itself, which served him endless amounts of content that fit his behavioural profile. The more he engaged with and shared racist content, the more the networks would feed him. This is the first crime of social media as an accomplice to mass murder in this event. The second crime is the live stream and how social media amplified this content and spread it like wildfire across the globe, which would inspire countless other white supremacists and terrorists to engage in their own lone wolf action and live stream it to the world.

As Brenton Tarrant drove towards the Al Noor mosque on the day of the shootings, he hit the red button on his Facebook Live stream. Minutes before this, he had emailed his 74-page manifesto to a mailing list of media and politicians, including New Zealand's prime minister Jacinda Ardern. Tarrant also shared links on Facebook, Twitter and 8Chan (the spin-off web forum of 4Chan). As viewers instantly started to tune into his livestream they saw and heard Tarrant driving while listening to songs such as "The British Grenadiers", a traditional British military marching song; and "Remove Kebab", a Serb nationalist and anti-Muslim propaganda music video cheering the genocidal Radovan Karadžić. Moments later, his massacre would begin and live-streamed 17 minutes of the shooting as he entered into the Mosque and indiscriminately started killing innocent people in cold blood. The video wasn't noticed by Facebook until 12 minutes after the live broadcast had ended. In a Facebook News statement on March 18th three days after the event the company made the following bullet point comments [4].

- "The video was viewed fewer than 200 times during the live broadcast. No users reported the video during the live broadcast. Including the views during the live broadcast, the video was viewed about 4000 times in total before being removed from Facebook."

- "The first user report on the original video came in 29 minutes after the video started, and 12 minutes after

4 Facebook Update on New Zealand https://about.fb.com/news/2019/03/update-on-new-zea-land/

the live broadcast ended."

• "Before we were alerted to the video, a user on 8chan posted a link to a copy of the video on a file-sharing site."

Facebook was trying to mitigate their role in facilitating a live view of the massacre being viewed by anyone at any time. Facebook said the automatic systems to spot propaganda or terrorist output was caught out in two ways with the Christchurch videos.

• First, it said, a "core community of bad actors" worked together to continually reupload edited copies of the video that were altered to defeat the detection systems.

• "Second, the way people shared the video, sometimes by recording clips shown on TV, made it harder to spot copies."

Guy Rosen, vice-president of integrity at Facebook, said in a blog that when users reported the video, they did not use terms or tags that would have prompted the social network to review it more quickly.

"The video was reported for reasons other than suicide,

and as such, it was handled according to different procedures," wrote Mr Rosen.

In total, 800 different variants of the video were found and blocked on Facebook. The live stream had been captured by many people, allowing for it to be copied and syndicated multiple times across multiple channels. The video was simultaneously uploaded to Facebook, YouTube, Instagram, LiveLeak, SnapChat, 8Chan, 4Chan, Twitter, and any other social media and web forum that showed interest. The video had been seeded via TOR file-sharing networks. It was unstoppable to suppress the sharing of this video. The more these networks tried to remove the video, the more times it was uploaded by a different user and account. And then the mainstream media got hold of the source video. While they didn't show the entire video, they did start airing on live TV clips from the video. This amplified the video even more so that more and more people went online to search for it. A video that had been seen less than 200 times when lives streamed now had a global audience of the entire planet as the news spread viral both on social media and through news media. To try and slow the spread of the sharing of this video, at least in New Zealand, it was classified as a criminal offence to distribute the film. The New Zealand Office of Film and Literature Classification classified the video as "objectionable", making it a criminal offence in the country to distribute, copy, or exhibit the video, with potential penalties of up to 14 years' imprisonment for an individual, or up to $100,000 in fines for a corporation [5]. At least eight people had been arrested for possessing or sharing the video or manifesto; most of their names have been suppressed either to prevent threats against them or in support of freedom of expression online [6].

It was too little, too late. The wrath of social media had been engaged and activated. The Livestream video of the Christchurch massacre would now inspire white supremacists worldwide, following in the footsteps of Norwegian Anders Behring Breivik, who Tarrant had directly named in his manifesto as a source for his inspiration. Social media had blood on its hands. And not just for facilitating the live-streaming and consequential viewing of the snuff video on demand. Social media had helped create and foster the hate and wrath within Tarrant, which would lead him to make the choices he made. We are now living in the era of what has been called performance crime. Stuart Bender of Curtin University in Perth noted that the use of live video as an integral part of the attacks "makes [them] a form of 'performance crime' where the act of video recording and/or streaming the violence by the perpetrator is a central component of the violence itself, rather than being incidental [7]."

5 OFLC Response to Christchurch – What You Can Do https://www.classificationoffice.govt.nz/news/latest-news/oflc-response-to-christchurch-what-you-can-do/
6 Warning over threats in Christchurch terror attack video prosecutions https://www.stuff.co.nz/national/christchurch-shooting/112051430/warning-over-threats-in-christchurch-terror-attack-video-prosecutions
7 'Thousands' of Christchurch shootings videos removed from YouTube, Google says https://www.stuff.co.nz/business/111330323/facebook-working-around-the-clock-to-block-christchurch-shootings-video

Christchurch was just the tipping point that caused global and political outrage against social media corporations, which forced them to try and take some action to clean up their mess. Jacinda Ardern, the Prime Minister of New Zealand, was even served the video herself and was disgusted and outraged that Facebook had served the video to her timeline. "I went onto social media to post information soon after the attack and it auto-played," Ardern told Stuff [8].

Before the Christchurch massacre, there were hundreds if not thousands of other live-streaming events that amount to nothing more than watching live snuff videos. Had facebook become that version of the top tier violence pornography depicted in David Cronenberg's film Videodrome? A quick glance back at the archives over the past five years of Facebook live will paint a very dark picture of the real-world Videodrome world of Social Media live streaming. Here are just a few examples.

- A Thai man filmed himself killing his 11-month-old daughter in two video clips posted on Facebook before committing suicide[9].

- Woman playing with guns shoots man while on Facebook Live[10].

8 Jacinda Ardern saw the Christchurch video and will try and stop something like that happening ever again https://www.stuff.co.nz/national/politics/112642551/jacinda-ardern-saw-the-christchurch-video-and-will-try-and-stop-something-like-that-happening-ever-again
9 Thai man broadcasts baby daughter's murder live on Facebook https://www.reuters.com/article/us-thailand-facebook-murder-idUSKBN17R1DG
10 Woman who shot man on Facebook Live sentenced to 15 years in prison https://www.fox26hou-

- Robert Godwin Sr., was killed when Steve Stephens shot the 74-year-old man at point-blank range whilst live streaming[11].

- Four people were charged in 2017 for the brutal beating and kidnapping of an 18-year-old man with special needs[12].

- A man in California live streamed himself firing at deputies in California. Sean Vasquez, 20, recorded himself loading a gun and then firing shots at officers[13].

- A 55-year-old North Carolina man who went to complain to police after a family member stole his cell phone ended up capturing his own murder[14].

- The shooting death of a man and a 2-year-old boy was streamed on Facebook, a violent display of the gunfire that has killed two children in Chicago [15].

ston.com/news/woman-who-shot-man-on-facebook-live-sentenced-to-15-years-in-prison
11 Cleveland shooting: Race to track down Ohio's 'Facebook shooter' before he can kill again https://
www.independent.co.uk/news/world/americas/cleveland-ohio-facebook-killer-shooter-steve-ste-
phens-robert-godwin-a7686771.html
12 Man gets 8 years after guilty plea in Chicago Facebook Live torture, beating https://abc7chicago.
com/chicago-hate-crime-torture-facebook-live/3713952/
13 Covina suspect shoots at deputies while recording Facebook Live https://abc7.com/sean-
vasquez-facebook-live-covina-shooting-los-angeles/1853113/
14 Suspected killer arrested in Facebook Live murder https://abc7news.com/facebook-live-murder-
streamed-on-social-media-homicide/3149536/
15 Toddler's Killing Is Captured on Facebook Live as City's Pain Plays on a Loop https://www.
nbcnews.com/news/us-news/chicago-violence-toddler-s-killing-captured-facebook-live-city-
s-n721286

- Police said they are searching for five to six men suspected of sexually assaulting a 15-year-old girl in an attack that was streamed on Facebook Live [16].

This list could go on and on. It is all there. Murder, rape, kidnapping, torture, assault, robbery, random killing, premeditated killing, racist attacks and terrorist attacks. Social media has created both a facilitator for our wrath and a way to instant infamy through the actions of our wrath. If you have been following and paying attention to your Facebook, you will have noticed that there used to be a Facebook Live button in your menu, which would take you to a global map. This map would show you in real-time all the people who were live-streaming publicly. It was an exciting experiment to see in real-time broadcasts from all around the world.

Most of these broadcasts were mundane. Yet a lot of them were political, and some of them had commercial reasons. In a post-Christchurch world, this map is no longer assessable on Facebook. Quietly removed from the interface and no longer a public-facing feature of the site. Any and all references to the original Christchurch massacre video have been removed from Facebook and all social media sites and censorship of the clip on Google search and YouTube. Of course, like anything that has

16 Suspected gang rape of Chicago teen streamed on Facebook Live https://eu.usatoday.com/story/news/2017/03/21/chicago-gang-rape-teen-streamed-facebook-live/99447884/

never been lives streamed or published online, the Christchurch video is still accessible and can be found through alternative channels. However, it is still an offence in many countries to re-share and distribute the video, and if you try to do this on your social media channels, you can be guaranteed to be instantly banned from their network. However, this won't stop the next terrorist massacre from being live-streamed online and making its way to global news feeds through mainstream media. While social media companies desperately try and stuff the genie back into the bottle, they are hopelessly positioned to stop the train they have let loose on the world. Their networks have driven the content of hate a polarisation; they have amplified our wrath and create the perfect storm of using questionable content to keep certain groups of people online and on the platform so they could generate revenue from serving adverts to them. Angry people click more. So the more wrath we feel, the more money social media companies make. The more we click, the angrier we become. Wrath is an essential component to the social media algorithm.

* * * * * *

INCELS

TERRORISM WHICH THREATENS us today is more likely to come from white supremacists, ultra-nationalists and involuntary celibates rather than emanating from Islamic extremists. This depends on your location, but according to the centre for strategic and international studies data set of terrorist incidents, the most significant threat likely comes from white supremacists. However, anarchists and religious extremists inspired by the Islamic State and al-Qaeda could also present a potential danger. We still live in the age of the War on Terror [1]. Yet in 2021, terror is more likely to come from someone who had spent the past few years festering on social media. They are now ready to publish their manifesto to go and commit mass murder with a selection of automatic weapons he had been collecting for that special day of wrath. Both Islamic terrorism and white supremacist terrorism have in common how they both use social media as a recruitment and propaganda wing of their respective armies. A 2013 report by the National Criminal Justice Reference Service for the U.S department of Justice [2] found that "the lone-wolf terrorist tends to broadcast his/her intention to commit violence, usually because they are acting out of a commitment to send a message through the attack." The lone-wolf terrorist is driven to commit acts of violence on behalf of a political or

1 The Escalating Terrorism Problem in the United States https://www.csis.org/analysis/escalating-terrorism-problem-united-states
2 Lone Wolf Terrorism in America https://www.ojp.gov/ncjrs/virtual-library/abstracts/lone-wolf-terrorism-america

religious ideology. Something even more sinister and entirely off the radar has emerged following lone-wolf operatives' style in the past few years. 'INCELS'.

An "involuntary celibate", AKA 'Incel' is a member of an online subculture of people who define themselves as unable to find a romantic or sexual partner despite desiring one. We live through the age of free to view online pornography of every fetish and nature to endless streams of social media Insta-babes and the era of the beautiful people. We right swipe our lives away on Tinder, bed-hopping from one easy mattress jump to another. The pressure for young men to find a girlfriend, let alone a life partner, has become even more complicated than before. With societies more focused on augmented reality filters and their image, relationships have suffered for young men, especially as it became harder to get laid in a society that is putting so much pressure on getting laid. Our advertising, popular culture and media constantly pressure people about the body beautiful while pushing a narrative of sex sells. The better you look, the more sex you will have. Social media sites let the lucky ones promote and showcase their relationship status while at the same time allowing good looking females free access to dating sites and services while men have to pay to play.

Alek Minassian killed 10 people by driving a van down a busy street in Toronto and ramming into anyone who happened to be in his way. He was a 'terrorist'. How do we know this? He told us. He told us through his Facebook posts as he publicly posted his allegiance to the "Incel Rebellion." This rebellion is a union of Incel's who self identify and group through social media, chat apps and forums. They are united in the belief that women are "shallow, vicious, and only attracted to hyper-muscular men." This is seen as an injustice to men like Minassian and others who identify as Incels. Their male uprising of the Incel Rebellion directly results from how women have treated them or not treated them in many of their cases; they have been unable to persuade anyone from the opposite sex to go to bed with them. Incel's resentment and hatred, misogyny, misanthropy, self-pity and self-loathing, racism, a sense of entitlement to sex, and the endorsement of violence against sexually active people are all perfectly justified. The Incel are, after all, the victim of women's shallowness according to the Incel's ideas. The incel rebellion community has been growing through social media, through open and very public channels, and through closed and private groups. In the case of Minassian he made his views very public by posting to Facebook minutes before he would commit his murderous rampage [3].Others had been more prolific on their multichannel posting and amplification of incel ideology. Four years before Alek Minassian's attack, Elliot Rodger, a 22-year-old student at the University of California, Santa Barbra, killed six people and wounded others before killing himself in his car. Alek Minassian

[3] Toronto van attack suspect declared 'Incel Rebellion' in chilling Facebook post https://abcnews. go.com/International/News/toronto-van-attack-suspect-declared-incel-rebellion-chilling/story?id=54718771&cid=social_fb_abcn&fbclid=IwAR2of03Eq2FwDVzOQoSYITN1shixyZ-a-hn9sbaYTy-FsZIWDklaBu-NAsMA

mentioned Elliot Rodger in his Facebook posts just before he committed his crimes. Praising Rodger as an inspiration to what he was just about to do. In several YouTube videos, a blog and a 137-page manifesto created before the 2014 rampage, Rodger moaned about his "loneliness", and he appeared angry why women were "repulsed" because he saw himself as an "ultimate gentleman." I remember, at the time, just after the shooting event, watching Elliot Rodger's videos via LiveLeak. He sat in his car usually at sunsets, and would calmly and coldly lay out his feelings in a manifesto style narrative. All of this being uploaded to YouTube and openly and publicly showcasing warning signs that this person was on the verge of doing something horrific. Elliot Rodger's video and rants were directly against women. Not individual women but all women. Anyone woman in his eyes was now a valid target and, in his view, would be a justifiable causality in what would become the start of the Incel Rebellion. The most genuine and present danger our modern western societies have faced in decades. Forget Al-Qaeda and ISIS for a moment. You have more chance of being run down and shot by a 20-year-old white male Incel or white supremacists than you have an Islamic terrorist, and especially it seems if you are a woman.

Misogyny and sexism are rampant on social media. Especially on Twitter but not exclusively to that channel. Just on Twitter, it is somewhat easier to hide behind a fake name and set up an almost untraceable account and off the grid, so to speak.

Threats of violence, rape and death are made against women on social media every second of every day. The volume of such content is staggering and frightening at the same time. During COVID-19, misogynistic attacks on women have only increased, primarily because more people were spending more timelines online and on social media due to the lockdown conditions. The Center on Gender Equity and Health, University of California San Diego, looked at Trends in online misogyny before and during the COVID-19 pandemic [4]. They conducted an analysis of Twitter data from five South-Asian countries. What they found was eye-opening.

- The percentage of tweets containing misogynistic content increased significantly in South Asia during the pandemic; a consistent and steady increase was observed particularly since July 2020.
- In addition to gendered slur words and abusive content, many misogynistic tweets focused on discrediting reports of violence against women and criticising feminist movements.
- Distinct peaks in the volume of misogynistic tweets were observed in response to specific events related to gender rights.

---

4 Trends in online misogyny before and during the COVID-19 pandemic: Analysis of Twitter data from five
South-Asian countries https://data2x.org/wp-content/uploads/2021/03/UCSD-Brief-3_BigDataGenderCOVID19SouthAsianMisogyny.pdf

"While digital spaces have amplified female voices, these platforms are also notoriously and increasingly infiltrated by hate speech, including misogynist comments. Our analysis indicates a significant increase in the prevalence of misogyny on Twitter in South Asia since the COVID-19 related lockdowns began. This is in line with global studies that have found an increase in different forms of hate speech related to race and ethnicity on social media by women. Digital hate speech can be viewed as a sanction, deployed to discourage changes in behaviour that are perceived to violate patriarchal norms.

Our findings suggest that hate speech in digital spaces proliferates following specific incidents related to conflict or crises. We find that the spikes in online abuse correspond with events related to feminist movements or gender rights across our nations of focus. Although seemingly obvious, this backlash is alarming given that such content discredits reports of violence and everyday discrimination experienced."

It's not just women in South-Asian countries who are experiencing this. This trend is prevalent worldwide, and Twitter is at the forefront of facilitating the abuse. Women all over the world are facing an endless onslaught of male wrath, thanks to social media. Female politicians seem to be at the forefront of social media abuse, with Twitter as the primary facilitator of and amplifier of male wrath. Flick Drummond is a Member of Parliament of the United Kingdom for the conservative party. She represents and is the elected member of parliament for Meon Valley since 2019. In April 2021, Drummond quit Twitter. "Like others, I have come off Twitter. There was no point in looking at comments designed to hurt one personally rather than deal with politics. If a woman raises her head above the parapet, it triggers even more abuse, so many wonder whether it is worth talking about a controversial topic. That is a stultifying discussion, especially given that the diversity of a woman's perspective is often helpful. We are tough as politicians, but we are also human beings. Many of us have families whom we want to protect as well as ourselves. I challenge every single person to confront this unacceptable behaviour. Otherwise, we will have to put further consequences in place to combat it." Drummond also cited The Fawcett Society's recent findings of a trend towards women not seeking to be elected into positions of power, with online abuse playing a factor [5]. UK female politicians are more acutely aware of the dangers to their safety than ever before. On June 16th 2016, Jo Cox, the Member of Parliament for Batley and Spen in West Yorkshire, was murdered in a knife attack by a 52-year-old man Thomas Mair. While Mair had proven links to neo-Nazi groups, and he shouted "Britain first" as he attacked Jo Cox, it could also be argued that Mair shows some similar traits with younger male Incels' he was also known to have had psychiatric problems. Jo Cox's murder on the streets of the UK had taken

---

5 WE NEED MORE WOMEN: URGENT ACTION NEEDED ON WOMEN'S REPRESENTATION https://www.fawcettsociety.org.uk/blog/we-need-more-women-urgent-action-needed-on-womens-representation

the BREXIT campaign into new and darker territory, whereupon people's wrath had started to overspill from online and social media threats and into real-world actions that had murderous consequences. Social media sites had facilitated and amplified the hatred and wrath projected towards Jo Cox and other female politicians like her and had done little to nothing to try and stop it. Member of Parliament for Birmingham Yardley Jess Philips even went as far as to accuse Twitter of 'colluding' with the social media users who made rape threats against her. Writing in the Daily Telegraph newspaper, she said: "I am currently living in a parallel universe where the idea of not raping me is the insult du jour. Here, not raping someone is what you do to the people that you find repellent. To see the attack of a pack on here, check out my mentions 600 odd notifications talking about my rape in one night. I think Twitter is dead. After all, I'm big enough, ugly enough and un-rapable enough to take it. If these were letters to my office, the police would currently befitting panic buttons and telling me to stay away. Yet Twitter appears willing to do absolutely nothing."

Jess Philips is not alone in her feelings that Twitter does nothing to protect its users from vile abuse that happens daily and even hourly. It has become the social media of choice for wrath. Wrath fuels the vast majority of Tweets and Twitter content as people react in real-time to events and situations with little time for reflection and thought. Twitter is created where it is too easy to create a fake account without much fear of getting caught if you take a few basic and simple steps to anonymise your identity. From there on in, you can set about abusing, threatening, stalking and harassing anyone, so you wish to do so. While Twitter offered a creative way to connect in a short form micro-blogging way, the site has become synonymous with racism, sexism, death threats and online abuse. It is the bluebird portal into a universe of wrath and a reflection of the world of women-hating men. However, as we will see later in this chapter, Twitter abuse is not just a male phenomenon. There is plenty of female wrath on social media, and Twitter is their social network of choice once again.

Social media should, in theory, be a safe place. If you control your privacy settings and carefully monitor who you publish to and who you allow to follow you, it can be limited to a social network of friends, family and peers. Yet, from the beginning social media networks set up their systems so your posts would be as open and as public as possible. It is up to you to navigate the complicated and 'user-unfriendly' interfaces that hide the majority of overly complex settings to ensure your profile is locked down, private and safe. Social media companies prefer if you post publicly and openly; this way, it feeds the algorithm more and can gather more and more data on more and more users. The publicly you post, the more people can reach and engage with you. The more controversial your opinions, the more hate and wrath you will create in response.

Angry people click more. So your wrath will spurn more wrath until your angry posts have made a vast amount of revenue for the social media companies by keeping users onsite and clicking. Thus allowing the social media company to serve more and more advertisements sponsored content into their feeds. The longer you stay on the platform per session, the more revenue you create for the network. The more wrath you feel, the longer you will allow your anger to spill out through your comments, reposts and re-shares of content justifies your wrath.

We can try and understand the incel state of mind. In the LUST chapter, we can see how social media has put so much pressure on the beautiful body. How social media algorithms promote the Instagram babe and the semi-naked beautiful bodies. There has always been pressure on young men to get laid; this is nothing new of the social media era. What is new is how the medium of social media ends up being the only thing that wants to fuck you. And not in a good way. Social media has amplified the feelings of wrath when it comes to the Incel state of mind. It has provoked and humiliated young men into feeling insecure and unhappy about themselves. While promoting and facilitating the perfect body image with an endless stream of models like girls who glow under their filtered social media reality of unrealistic images, bunny ears and cat whiskers faces. Young men have found refuge in video gaming in online communities and saw the endless stream of free pornography as an outlet for their sexual frustrations and fantasies. As pornography got more violent and more incestual, so the wrath against women grew. The next chapter of ENVY will also link back to the Incel's mindset. Social media and the seven deadly sins could be applied to each and every sin to the Incel. All behaviours and sins are present in this mindset. For each one and each example, we can see clearly how social media has played a role in facilitating and or radicalising their individual to a state where they can commit mass murder.

The #MeToo movement began a fightback for women to once again share their stories and speak their truths of the constant misogyny, harassment and rape they face daily. As the onslaught against women through social media grew, so did the ability for women to share their stories with one another and gain collective courage to start to speak out about it. No part of mainstream social media can be considered a safe space for women. If you are a woman on social media, you can expect many unsolicited dick pics, rape threats and general sexist and misogynistic comments made towards you. Unwanted messages in your inbox. The feeling that no matter what you do or where you go, be it in real-world situations or online and social media, you will be catcalled and made a sexual object by a man, if not once but multiple times each and every day. It could be said that the #MeToo movement started in America and spread rapidly around the world. Stemming from the horrific abuse of actors at the hands of Harvey Weinstein representing all those other seedy film producers and Hollywood types who have used the casting couch as a means to pressure women into sexual activities for the promise of financial payback or starring roles in the latest big-budget movie. Failing that to just threaten and scare women into sexual acts through the mysticism of the abuser's fame and often fortune in a Hollywood controlled for decades by its ideology of it's not what you know but who you blow. Yet as more women spoke out about it, this tipping was going to actually make a change, and attitudes of the past no longer have a place in modern society. The rape of women, and men, are not accepted. Equality for all is universally understood as the way forward for modern liberal and progressive democracies. The patriarchal dominance of yesteryears is starting to be rebalanced as feminism rightly fights for the primary and most simplistic human rights that women worldwide have the opportunity to obtain. Finally, #MeToo is caught up to the advertising industry, which is the middle man when we consider our addiction to social media. It is widely known, understood and accepted that the advertising industry is one of the most sexist, misogynistic and downright dirty industries in the world regarding how it treats and portrays women. An industry dominated at the higher levels, especially when men consider the creative direction and executive management level. As is the same for most brands and corporations that employ the services of ad agencies. Men dominate the C level and board member positions in marketing, sales and communication. Yet, it has taken us almost five years since the #MeToo movement hit the mainstream consciousness for people to start talking about the situation in the advertising industry, both in ad agencies and on the client side. On July 4th 2021 campaigner Zoe Scaman published a blog article titled "MAD MEN. FURIOUS WOMEN"[6]. In the article, Scaman highlighted some of her own shocking and horrific experiences working in advertising. From a young 18-year-old intern all the way through to her current time at the age of 36. 18 years of misogyny, rape, sexual abuse, inequality and downright disgusting behaviour at all levels from the men who work in the industry and the ad agencies she worked for. And that wasn't the end of it. Joe Scaman had collected many other similar stories from many other women in advertising[7]. When writing this, there were also many hundreds of comments under her blog article recounting similar experiences. It seemed that the creative and advertising industries were quite possibly one of the most disgusting and dangerous workplaces for women to be. The endless tales of rape, unwanted sexual advances, meeting room sexism and misogyny made the scale of #MeToo in Hollywood is just a teaser campaign when considering the evidential scale of #MeToo within the advertising industry. Joe Scaman specifically called out social media in her article and particularly again Twitter.

"I'm now 36 and, having a built a profile on Twitter, my

6 Mad Men. Furious Women. https://zoescaman.substack.com/p/mad-men-furious-women
7 Advertising sector has #MeToo moment as blog sparks women's anger https://www.theguardian.com/media/2021/jul/15/advertising-sector-has-metoo-moment-as-blog-sparks-womens-anger

daily sojourns on the platform bring a healthy dose of reply guys and mansplaining, but also unsolicited advances, dick pics, rape threats, and occasionally, threats on my life too. And when I raise the issue, the response is often 'why don't you just get off of Twitter', as if the only solution to the abuse directed at me is to punish myself - to run away, to cower in a corner, to abandon the audience I've built and the new business pipeline it's created."

Joe Scaman is right. Why should she leave Twitter? She shouldn't have to. Why are so many women told to just leave the site or feel that they have no option other than to quit social media? Indeed it's Twitter who should remove the abusers? Yet as we have seen in the chapter LUST, Twitter has a way of supporting abusers more than it does to support the abused. As social media and the advertising industry are now hand-in-glove, one can't exist without the other; we can see how this rapist culture and misogynistic attitudes seep through all social networks and prop up and support the INCEL mindset.

It's been well documented that Facebook was founded on a "frat-house vibe" [8]. Facebook is founded on sexism. Facebook HQ murals commissioned by Mark Zuckerberg from street artist David Choe highlighted this in all its gory detail. Sprawling murals contained grotesque and profane images throughout the offices as described by journalist Steven Levy. "It was like as if Playboy had commissioned Hieronymus Bosch to tag a

---

8 Sexism at Facebook Is What Made It Facebook https://www.theatlantic.com/technology/archive/2012/07/sexism-facebook-what-made-it-facebook/326191/

subway car [9]." The murals depicted many large-breasted women and sexualised imagery. There was also graffiti in the women's bathroom showing a woman defecating. Much to the delight of the male workers of Facebook, not appreciated by the female workers, many of whom would blow the whistle on the sexist and misogynistic environment that working at Facebook was. If we consider how Facebook was created, one could argue that it was through an act of Incel Rebellion. Mark Zuckerberg's idea for FaceMash is explained in his white man angry blog post. The concept for FaceMash coming directly after Zuckerberg had been stood up on a date by a fellow student.

> "I'm a little intoxicated, not gonna lie. So what if it's not even 10pm and it's a Tuesday night? What? The Kirkland facebook is open on my computer desktop and some of these people have pretty horrendous facebook pics. I almost want to put some of these faces next to pictures of farm animals and have people vote on which is more attractive. It's not such a great idea and probably not even funny, but Billy comes up with the idea of comparing two people from the facebook, and only sometimes putting a farm animal in there. Good call Mr. Olson! I think he's onto something [10]."

9 Facebook: the Inside Story, by Steven Levy https://www.penguinrandomhouse.com/books/551043/facebook-by-steven-levy/
10 MARK ZUCKERBERG'S FACEMASH BLOG POSTS https://www.socialstudent.co.uk/mark-zuckerbergs-facemash-blog-posts-part-1/

As we can see, Facebook was created from an act of wrath by an insecure white 20-year-old male who was angry at a woman for not wanting to date him. It is no wonder why rage against women is personified and prolific on our social networks today. Is Mark Zuckerberg actually the founding father of Incels?

* * * * * *

SOCIAL JUSTICE WARRIORS

IT'S IMPORTANT TO say at the front of this chapter that I am an atheist and apolitical. I don't believe in any gods or religion, just as I don't believe in any political parties of their ideologies. I will be writing about both the left and right of politics, which focuses on British and American politics in terms of social media and social justice warriors. I don't have a political viewpoint nor a political agenda in what I say. I am just trying to make a viewpoint from the seven deadly sins of social media and the sin of wrath, which I feel is one of the most toxic sins that dominates the vast majority of social media interaction.

With the growth of social media comes the stampede of Social Justice Warriors. And while I do promote a world in which social justice is prevalent, I do not wish to be part of the social justice culture that occurs on social media. It is driven by WRATH. The road to hell is pathed with good intentions. While online social justice campaigns may start with good intentions, they often lead to difficult situations. Social media has given people the opportunity to complain easily and to do it directly. Suppose you are disappointed in a product, brand and or customer experience. In that case, you can now tell your feelings directly to the company's CEO by finding them on Twitter or LinkedIn or any other social media channel where they may have a presence. You can let them know directly how you feel. As I have worked in community management and social media customer service for many years, I can tell you, CEO's and brand managers are accurately aware of what people tweet and say on social media about their brands, products and companies. All it takes is literally just one person to send a few angry tweets, and meetings of PR managers, social media managers and marketing execs are called to the table to discuss how to deal with it. Good social media and community managers know how to deal with complaints and angry social media messages. They can flip them around and play with them and turn them into MEME-like content or even viral posts without damaging the brand. However, most social media managers don't know what kind of tone of voice to use or how to talk to others in an internet language style, so their replies or mostly lack of replies can go on to create a PR crisis and a media shitstorm. Especially if you screw up your content and fall foul of the latest and most recently social justice warrior campaigns. If you upset a social justice warrior, you can be assured that your career and life will become a living hell. So what exactly is a 'Social Justice Warrior' (SJW)? Merriam-Webster describes them as follows. "Social Justice Warrior and SJW are typically used with sardonic application, referring to a person who is seen as overly enthusiastic about issues of fairness in the treatment of matters of race, gender, or identity" [1].

A SJW doesn't have to be just focused on the issues of

---

1 Words We're Watching Social Justice Warrior https://www.merriam-webster.com/words-at-play/what-does-social-justice-warrior-sjw-mean

race, gender or identity. There is plenty more to be outraged against. And I would even consider the "anti-political correct" brigade as a form of SWJ. Similar in their wrath, online and social media behaviour and overall agenda to try and use social media as a way to bully people or deny them their right to thought and expression by getting them removed from social media or making them feel so bombarded and harassed that they just leave. It is what has been termed as cancel culture.

Social Justice Warriors have also found themself becoming newsworthy. By actively perusing and status of SJW, they can become an online celebrity, an influencer or even a campaign figurehead and revolutionary leader. I say revolutionary as if we deep dive into the world of Social Justice Warriors and their origins, we will see they have a background incoming from the far left of the political-ideological spectrum. Where SJW's have been most active has been in the USA and the UK. These two cultures have enough in common regarding their left-wing politics and their cultural identities and liberal democracy challenges.

I believe in the UK, there is a link between the increase in Social Justice Warriors with the rise of the Labour party youth movement of Momentum. Momentum was founded in 2015 by Jonathan Lansman, a veteran British political activist. Lansman was a key player in Jeremy Corbyn's campaigns and a member of the all-powerful Labour Party's National Executive Committee. Earlier in his activist career, Lansman had worked for both Tony

Benn and Michael Meacher. As a political activist and strategist, Lansman created the biggest political youth movement in modern British history. Digitally savvy and social media friendly, Momentum would unleash its Social Justice Warriors out into the British public and the global cyberspace of social media to support and bring home the vote for Jeremy Corbyn as the next Prime Minister of the UK. Well, we know now how that worked out. Boris Johnson won the 2019 Conservative Party leadership election and became Prime Minister on 23 July 2019. The Conservatives swept aside Labour in its traditional heartlands to win a commons majority [2]. Labour and the leadership of Corbyn had crashed and burnt, suffering the most humiliating defeat in the Labour party's history. No amount of MEME's and cancel culture rhetoric from Momentum would turn the tide. It looked like now Labour would never get back into power again unless in some form of collation government. Was Jeremy to blame or this? Mostly. Yet, so the blame must be put on Lansman and his Momentum movement. The damage done by the Social Justice Warriors lead to the spotlight turning onto the rampant, and abhorrent Anti Semitism which was festering deep within the Labour party with the centre of this racist abscess buried deep within Momentum activists. Lansman, Jewish and brought up in an Orthodox Jewish family, soon found himself trying to explain his way out of a tricky situation. His party and movement were being accused of the most rampant anti-Semitism. Lansman was a self-proclaimed Atheist, but he still did follow Jewish holidays. Lansman was interviewed by The Jewish Chronicle in January 2016. He was asked about attitudes to Israel in the Labour Party and the attitudes of Jews towards it: "Yes, of course the vast majority of British Jews are supportive of Israel as a Jewish state – and actually so is Jeremy – but they are far from supportive of all aspects of what is currently happening there", he said. "I think Jews in Britain want peace too. I think Jeremy's message of fairness for the Palestinians is not something that will be rejected by the Jewish community.

Fast forward to 2019 and Lansman was having to admit that he thought Labour had a hardcore problem with anti-semitism and that it was widespread within the party [3]. And this was all starting to showcase itself through social media. Momentum activists and Labour party members were not even trying to hide their feelings towards Jews and Israel with even the Momentum treasurer ended up suspended from the Labour party for comments he made on social media [4].

Lansman's incredible work in creating a social media savvy and youthful political movement was fresh and new in British politics. His Facebook strategy was highly effective and could engage and activate tens of thousands of followers with

3 Labour has widespread problem with antisemitism – Momentum founder https://www.theguard-ian.com/politics/2019/feb/25/labour-has-widespread-problem-with-antisemitism-momen-tum-founder-jon-lansman
4 Labour politician and former Momentum treasurer suspended from party over 'anti-Semitic post' https://www.standard.co.uk/news/london/momentum-labour-councillor-suspended-antisemi-tism-post-b130875.html

viral MEME that had clear calls to action [5]. However, it started crumbling and falling apart as the public began to see how toxic the Momentum Social Justice Warriors had become. This was amplified by the right-leaning media and Conservative party activists who were ready to pounce on any signs of SJW slip-ups and aggressive online and social media behaviour. Of course, not all members of the Labour party and Momentum are anti-Semites. Not all of them are revolutionary communists. However, some of them are the ones who made their voices the loudest and amplified through their actions on social media. They allowed their personal and political wrath to cloud their judgements, and they used social media as a way to attack any and all opposition to their own ideas and ideology in a rather thuggish and aggressive manner. They were given space with the party and the movement to dominate the narrative as their posts, and content on social media would 'drive engagement and increase reach'. Angry people click more, and nothing seems angrier than a Labour party supporter posting on social media. While the left of politics is supposed to be inclusive of all people and ideas, you will often find that left-leaning activists are the most intolerable of people who have different opinions from their own. Yet, there are many examples of this from the right of the political spectrum. Right-wing and conservative / Republican activists are also highly active on social media. The rise of Social

---

5 Understanding Labour's ingenious campaign strategy on Facebook https://blogs.lse.ac.uk/politicsandpolicy/explaining-labours-facebook-success/

Justice Warriors has inflamed and motivated right-wing activists to become even more active on social media to counterbalance and argue the toss. The resulting situation is polarisation. The majority of online and social media conversation around politics is highly polarised. There is no middle ground.

A decade ago, Eli Pariser coined the term "filter bubble" which he narrowly defined as a situation in which algorithms skew the variety of information we get online in favour of stuff we like. At the time, he worried that might lead to political polarisation through less exposure to divergent viewpoints. However, polarisation in its self is not directly a result of social media alone. It is prevalent in societies long before the internet and computers with their algorithms were unleashed upon us.

Marc A. Smith is a sociologist specialising in the social organisation of online communities and computer-mediated interaction. Smith leads the Connected Action consulting group and lives and works in Silicon Valley, California. Connected Action (www.connectedaction.net) applies social science methods in general and social network analysis techniques to enterprise and Internet social media usage. He is the co-editor, with Peter Kollock, of Communities in Cyberspace (Routledge), a collection of essays exploring the ways identity, interaction, and social order develop in online groups. Smith received a B.S. in International Area Studies from Drexel University in Philadelphia in 1988, an M. Phil. in social theory from Cambridge University in 1990, and a Ph.D. in Sociology from UCLA in 2001. He is an affiliate faculty at the Department of Sociology at the University of Washington and the College of Information Studies at the University of Maryland. Smith is a Distinguished Visiting Scholar at the Stanford University Media-X program. I asked Marc what he thought about Eli Parisers term filter bubble. If social media algorithms are to blame for the growth in political polarisation, we see in the world today. Here follows our conversation.

RW: Firstly I asked Marc if the recent hyper-partisan presidential election in the USA was an example of the "filter bubble" and if it could be the reason for the storming of the US Capitol?

MS: "Let me start with saying that Epistemology is the study of how we know what we know. Tribal epistemology is the idea that we believe what we believe based on our need to be members in groups. Groups demand members have certain beliefs in order to become and remain a member. Groups create all kinds of beliefs, some of which may even be accurate. Beliefs are propagated via exposure, repetition, endorsement, and sanctions. Beliefs like "democracy" are easy to interpret in different ways. All action is motivated by belief and all collective actions are motivated by shared beliefs. The insurrection was motivated by a shared set of beliefs about election integrity, grievances, and encouragement from public officials [6]. When faced with demographic changes that will block conservative majorities, redefining who is allowed to participate in politics is a clear strategy."

RW: Do you think that the "filter bubble" has created even greater polarisation between voters in American politics? And if so to what extent is social media responsible if at all?

MS: "Polarisation is high in many nations where there is growing demographic and culture demand for change. To block these shifts, incompatible "realities" are being constructed and maintained. These kinds of divisions predate social media (Reformation, for example). Social media does have a role, mostly as a conduit for previous forms of epistemological conflicts, with some added features based on its novel qualities. Speed, cost, scale, search-ability, remix-ability, mobile access, sensors, and machine learning are all real unique additions to the cultural landscape. But they join an existing process of struggle over the definition

6 The Zello Tapes: The Walkie-Talkie App Used During The Insurrection https://www.wnycstudios. org/podcasts/otm/segments/zello-tapes-walkie-talkie-app-used-during-insurrection-on-the-me-dia

of reality. Antonio Gramsci asked similar questions [7]. False consciousness, ideology, propaganda and indoctrination are all long established techniques for establishing a collective definition of reality, hierarchy, goals, allies, and enemies. The new tools do change some of the dynamics."

RW: Are you able to map and visually track examples of polarisation on Social Media through the network graph? If yes, how do you do it?

MS: "We can use network analysis and visualisation to map and gain an overview of social media discussions, including for topics that lack broad consensus. For example, antivaxx [8].

RW: To what extent can social media influence real world situations, events and ultimately democracies and the elections of presidents?

MS: "Social media is the latest way we tell each other what's going on. It has distinct structures that are distinct from prior forms of media. Social media creates larger populations of people with shared

7 Antonio Gramsci Wikipedia https://en.wikipedia.org/wiki/Antonio_Gramsci
8 NodeXL gallery - The graph represents a network of 9,523 Twitter users whose tweets in the requested range contained "antivaxx" http://nodexlgraphgallery.org/Pages/Graph.aspx?-graphID=258580

interests and within these populations fewer people become prominent because previous barriers have been removed. Social media makes the promise that all may speak. However, many people assume this also means that all may be heard. This is probably not the case. 93% of all tweets never get a reply for example. Social media and the internet are an electronic "nervous system" but it is not an electronic immune system. The removal of all gatekeepers has allowed suppressed voices to be heard, but it has also allowed fringe voices to also gain an audience. The gatekeeper is now who can craft attractive messages that amplify confirmation bias. These messages can certainly impact politics. Public perceptions are critical and very malleable. Should we wear masks? Should we get the shot? Who should bear responsibility for grave failures of government responses? People are mostly low information on most topics. No one is fully expert on all matters of relevance to the nation. We are mostly influenced by what we hear and see others do. This is a great example of how a few people in your network can be perceived as representing a majority. I think back to previous kinds of technical innovations and the history of their negative externalities and the development of mitigations. Steam boilers were once new and they had a nasty habit of exploding [9]. Cars have a long history of safety equipment slowly added to address their lethal qualities [10]. Similarly, many human aggregations require infrastructures for maintenance. Like London's rise and fall in population until it finally built a sewer system [11]. Metaphorically, social media is a young technology that has so far not had much mitigation innovation. I propose that we need such systems to shape what "trends" on social media along with better tools to evaluate and filter content [12]."

HE SHE THEM GENDER PRONOUNS

Another example of where Social Justice Warriors have exploded with wrath is transgender and non-binary. The subject has become so toxic that it has reached the point of civil court actions and police interventions due to death threats and aggressive behaviour that has been alleged to amount to stalking and harassment. There are many examples of where social media confrontations have escalated to such wrath and hateful levels of discourse. The campaign against British author J K Rowling being of the most publicised of these events. The Harry Potter

9 List of boiler explosions Wikipedia https://en.wikipedia.org/wiki/List_of_boiler_explosions?wprov=sfti1
10 Automotive safety Wikipedia https://en.wikipedia.org/wiki/Automotive_safety?wprov=sfti1
11 London sewerage system Wikipedia https://en.wikipedia.org/wiki/London_sewerage_system?wprov=sfti1
12 Let's pick our own social media editors https://www.smrfoundation.org/2021/07/06/lets-pick-our-own-social-media-editors/

author is very active on social media, Twitter being her channel of choice. Like many other authors, Rowling prefers the short form textual style of Twitter. It allows writers of her skill and ability to reply in a medium that is their specialism, words. The short format of tweets also allows highly skilled wordsmiths to craft impactful and often humorous responses in as few words as possible.

Interestingly enough, I find that lawyers and barristers also prefer Twitter for this exact same reason. It allows them to use their intellect and writing skills in powerful short verses and responses. In many ways, this is why Twitter is a powerful and valuable social media for the literate. However, for the illiterate and general masses, words, like arrows, can't be taken back once fired. Many people don't know how to handle their own words with care or understand the consequences of their meaning and contexts.

On June 6, 2020, JK Rowling retweeted an op-ed piece that discussed "people who menstruate," apparently taking issue with the fact that the story did not use the word women. "'People who menstruate.' I'm sure there used to be a word for those people. Someone help me out. Wumben? Wimpund? Woomud [13]?"

The Tweet caused an outraged response from SJW and Trans activists and would put into motion an endless Tweetstorm of confrontation between Rowling and the SJW activists. Rowling offended Tran activists; she also offended many women who no

---

13 @jk_rowling Tweet June 6th 2020 https://twitter.com/jk_rowling/status/1269382518362509313

longer menstruate due to menopause or other medical conditions. However, rather than drop it and move on, J K Rowling decided to take on the battle and continue her fight for what she sees as an issue of Women's rights. Rowling went on to write about her thoughts on this subject in much more detail. The more she wrote and shared on social media, the more wrath grew against her. To the point where even celebrities and former stars of her own creation, the Harry Potter movie turned against her. Daniel Radcliffe, Emma Watson, Rupert Grint, and Eddie Redmayne all started to speak out against Rowling's views. Masses of her fans declared boycotts against her books and hardcore Harry Potter fans, to which there are tens if not hundreds of millions of them, who were once children in love with her stories, were now young adults aghast at her views on transgenderism.

While J K Rowling was someone who had supported transgender rights, the way she used and expressed herself on social media created the backlash against her. She tweeted in great detail, trying to clarify her view without realising all she was doing was enraging the SJW even further and just adding more fuel to their wrath.

"If sex isn't real, there's no same-sex attraction. If sex isn't real, the lived reality of women globally is erased. I know and love trans people, but erasing the concept of sex removes the ability of many to meaningfully discuss their lives. It isn't hate to speak the truth," Rowling tweeted [14]. "The idea that women like

14 @jk_rowling Tweet June 7th 2020 https://twitter.com/jk_rowling/status/1269389298664701952

me, who've been empathetic to trans people for decades, feeling kinship because they're vulnerable in the same way as women— i.e., to male violence—'hate' trans people because they think sex is real and has lived consequences—is a nonsense. I respect every trans person's right to live any way that feels authentic and comfortable to them. I'd march with you if you were discriminated against on the basis of being trans. At the same time, my life has been shaped by being female. I do not believe it's hateful to say so."

By June 10th 2020, J K Rowling had decided to drop the short format of Twitter and use her own website and blog platform to write in greater detail to explain her views [15]. It was too late, the wrath of SJW's had been activated, and now J K Rowling would start to receive the full force of social media anger. Death threats soon arrived in her inbox as well as threats of rape, and other forms of physical and metal harm [16]. The Social Justice Warriors and especially the transgender activists are unforgiving once they have set their sites onto a target they wish to destroy. Regardless of someone else's point of view opinion, if they become activated and outraged your freedom of expression, right to speech and your own thoughts are no longer acceptable to them and you must be de-platformed and removed from social media as well as your books taken off the

15 J.K. Rowling Writes about Her Reasons for Speaking out on Sex and Gender Issues https://www.jkrowling.com/opinions/j-k-rowling-writes-about-her-reasons-for-speaking-out-on-sex-and-gender-issues/
16 Here are the death threats and harassment JK Rowling has been receiving. Including abuse from verified accounts. https://twitter.com/Dataracer117/status/1272737061703790592

shelves and ultimately erased from history [17].

J K Rowling is not the only writer and thinker who has fallen foul of Transgender and Social Justice Warrior wrath. Father Ted and IT Crowd creator and writer Graham Linehan found himself embroiled in Twitter spats with trans activists, which saw him having the fight all be it unjustified civil proceedings against himself after being given a warning for harassment [18]. It is essential to say that case brought against Linehan by the trans activist and serial litigator Stephanie Hayden dropped her High Court claim against him [19]. Hayden has a well-publicised track record of using legal means to silence users' critiques on Twitter that s/he takes offence to. This is a prime example of an SJW who basks in the social media spotlight and uses wrath and anger as a means of constant engagement and interaction.

Canadian professor of psychology, clinical psychologist Jordan Peterson shot to fame through his use of social media. His YouTube channel has hundreds of hours of videos of his lectures and classes. His views have caught the attention of young men all around the world. He is the author of many psychology books and what he calls his 12 rules for life. One of his significant debate subjects is Postmodernism and identity politics and his views on gender identity, which pitched him against the wrath

17 Bookshop refuses to stock JK Rowling novels over 'transphobia' furore https://www.smh.com.au/national/bookshop-refuses-to-stock-jk-rowling-novels-over-transphobia-furore-20200918-p55x20.html
18 Father Ted writer Graham Linehan given harassment warning https://www.bbc.com/news/uk-45777689https://www.bbc.com/news/uk-45777689
19 Transgender lawyer drops case against Father Ted writer https://www.rollonfriday.com/news-content/transgender-lawyer-drops-case-against-father-ted-writer

of Social Justice Warriors in North America and eventually around the world. Peterson suggests that universities are mainly responsible for a wave of political correctness that has appeared in North America and Europe [20], saying that he had watched the rise of political correctness on campuses since the early 1990s. Peterson believes the humanities have become corrupt and less reliant on science, in particular sociology. He contends that "proper culture" has been undermined by "post-modernism and neo-Marxism [21]." The fight and wrath against Peterson's point of view got so intense that student activists throughout North America lobbied and protested to ensure he was removed from campus and never invited to speak at their universities again. Of course, this helped propel Peterson to worldwide attention and rather than silence him, the Social Justice Warriors pushed him to become the best selling author and a guest speaker at events worldwide. Their wrath had rather than shut him down; it had amplified him into a global academic celebrity. He appeared on every news debate show and was invited to speak at major events and institutions worldwide. And quite rightly so. As you may disagree with what someone has to say, try and stop them from saying it or speaking their thoughts and truths is the true evil and exemplification of wrath that puts Social Justice Warriors on par with fascists.

---

20 Jordan Peterson and the trolls in the ivory tower https://www.theglobeandmail.com/news/national/education/jordan-peterson-university-of-toronto-free-speech-crowdfunding/article35174379/
21 Jordan Peterson and the transgender wars https://www.spectator.co.uk/article/jordan-peterson-and-the-transgender-wars

A final example of someone feeling the wrath of institutional Social Justice Warrior mentality is journalist Suzanne Moore. SJW ideology and mentality have spread within institutions, and non more obvious is that of the Guardian newspaper in the UK. Once a stalwart of protecting differing opinions, it has become nothing more than a facilitator of Social Justice Warrior behaviour by its leadership and editorial standards. Suzanne Moore is an award-winning columnist and journalist. She won the Orwell Prize in 2019. Moore has written for Marxism Today, The Mail on Sunday, Daily Mail, The Independent, The Guardian, and the New Statesman during her career.

In March 2020, Moore published an opinion piece in The Guardian, titled "Women must have the right to organise. We will not be silenced" [22]. The Guardian received a letter, with over 200 signatories, which rejected Moore's alleged implication that "advocating for trans rights poses a threat to cisgender women". The letter was signed by politicians such as Siân Berry, Christine Jardine, Nadia Whittome and Zarah Sultana, writers and journalists including Ash Sarkar and Reni Eddo-Lodge. The newspaper published the letter alongside others received in response to the article [23]. Needless to say, the wrath and outrage against Moore were rapidly forthcoming. In September 2020, The Telegraph wrote that Moore "had to have police protection

22 Women must have the right to organise. We will not be silenced https://www.theguardian.com/society/commentisfree/2020/mar/02/women-must-have-the-right-to-organise-we-will-not-be-silenced
23 Differing perspectives on transgender rights https://www.theguardian.com/society/2020/mar/04/differing-perspectives-on-transgender-rights

some years back as a result of voicing an unpopular opinion, and she has been deluged with abuse, rape and death threats online, even threats to rape her children." For voicing her views on gender, Moore had been subjected to vile threats of abuse by the Twitter social justice warriors and the transgender activists. By 16 November 2020, Moore announced she had left The Guardian. Moore went on to write a very in-depth article on Unherd, which would explain her reasons for leaving The Guardian. As an insight to what has happened behind the scenes of the newspaper and how the editorial decisions were being made in the vein of Social Justice Warriors rather than facilitating and supporting journalistic opinions and free speech of its writers [24].

The SJW's had taken yet another scalp. Or at least they had thought. Yet it was Moorse decision to quite the paper based on her principles rather than any actions or protests by the SJW's. However, they had made her life intolerable, and their constant wrath in the form of rape and death threats became too much for Moore to handle as it would for anyone who finds themselves on the end of such a barrage of online and social media hate.

Social Justice Warriors and fuelled by wrath. Wrath drives the fire in their hearts. While they may start with good intentions and want to try and make the world a better place, how social media amplifies and polarises issues, debates and situations mean that it is very confrontational and often ends with threats

24 Why I had to leave The Guardian. If you were bullied by 338 colleagues, what would you do? https://unherd.com/2020/11/why-i-had-to-leave-the-guardian/

to people's lives. Wrath spills over into violence and anti-social behaviour. Social media companies are unable to protect the users and communities on their platforms from abuse.

Moreover, the services and functions of the sites only encourage and enable abusers to target, harass and threaten people. The algorithm's echo chamber loop only entrenches people's views into polarised points of view; rather than allowing and supporting debate of differing viewpoints, they embed people into one closed hive mind. This is a dangerous outcome for humanity as censorship of debate and allowing people to have a differing point of view can only lead to the kinds of ideologies that we saw in the earthly 20th century. The road to hell is paved with good intentions. The road to fascism is pathed with angry tweets.

* * * * * *

TROLLING FOR LOL'S

Trolling has become an art form. Mostly it's harmless fun, especially in the online and social gaming communities. Yet sometimes trolling turns out to be something nasty. There is a vast amount of wrath within us. Social media allows us to quickly identify, target, and attack people with our wrath from the comfort of our homes and without anyone ever knowing who was doing it. Or so they may think. It is not always the case, as we shall see. Many trolls have been caught, their real identities have been outed, and criminal proceedings have followed. Some were found guilty, some got away with it.

The word trolling can often be misused. For example, it is often used out of context and in the form of retort. If someone disagrees with you and you have a different point of view, well, the easiest way to try and shut that down on social media is just to accuse that person of trolling you. You try to gaslight or devalue their point of view by making out that their criticism isn't valid as the reason for it is not genuine. This, of course, is something you will see and hear of a lot of when you look deeper into the Social Justice Warrior communities, as we have mentioned previously in this chapter. Where trolling gets nasty is when it becomes an organised and systematic campaign against someone, which often takes the form of harassment, bullying and stalking.

At 2.29pm on 29 July 2013, Isabella Sorley said on Twitter:

"Me doing something when tired only leads to one thing, me loosing [sic] my temper, but I'm sure sleep and wine will sort me out later." Twelve hours later, between 2.25am and 2.55am, she sent six tweets to two people: feminist writer Caroline Criado-Perez, who was campaigning for a woman to be featured on the £10 note, and Labour MP Stella Creasy, who supported the campaign. The tweets said: "Fuck off and die...you should have jumped in front of horses, go die; I will find you and you don't want to know what I will do when I do... kill yourself before I do; rape is the last of your worries; I've just got out of prison and would happily do more time to see you berried; seriously go kill yourself! I will get less time for that; rape?! I'd do a lot worse things than rape you [1]." By January of 2014, Isabella Sorley and her co-accused John Nimmo were jailed by Judge Howard Riddle for abusing feminist campaigner Caroline Criado-Perez on Twitter. Sentencing Ms Sorley, of Akenside Hill, Newcastle-upon-Tyne, to 12 weeks in prison and Mr Nimmo, of South Shields, Tyne and Wear, to eight weeks it was "hard to imagine more extreme threats". This was an important landmark in bringing social media tolls to justice. The threats made to Caroline Criado-Perez had been described by the judge as "life-changing". The abuse she received due to the wrathful campaign of hate had impacted her health and her mental well-being. However, the law hadn't always been so clear when it came to trolling and it was often applied in confusing,

---

1 This Is What It's Like To Go To Prison For Trolling https://www.buzzfeed.com/patricksmith/isabella-sorley-john-nimmo-interview

and inconsistent ways [2]. Some campaigners were calling for new laws to be created to deal with trolling [3]. Existing laws, if used correctly, would be more than sufficient in dealing with all forms of harassment. In the United Kingdom, contributions made to the Internet are covered by the Malicious Communications Act 1988 and Section 127 of the Communications Act 2003, under which jail sentences were, until 2015, limited to a maximum of six months. In October 2014, the UK's Justice Secretary, Chris Grayling, said that "Internet trolls" would face up to two years in jail, under measures in the Criminal Justice and Courts Bill that extend the maximum sentence and time limits for bringing prosecutions. The House of Lords Select Committee on Communications had earlier recommended against creating a specific offence of trolling. Sending messages which are "grossly offensive or of an indecent, obscene or menacing character" is an offence whether they are received by the intended recipient or not. Several people have been imprisoned in the UK for online harassment.

As I write this book today, many tens of people have been sent to prison for acts of 'trolling' on social media. These acts of trolling always step into the arena of wrath and are hate-filled, threatening and harassing by nature. Whereas social media companies say they do all they can to protect their users and offer clear community guidelines and means of reporting abuse,

2 Trolls of the testimonial page of Georgia Varley faced no prosecution due to misunderstandings of the legal system in the wake of the term trolling being popularised. https://www.liverpoolecho.co.uk/liverpool-news/local-news/2012/01/14/georgia-varley-inspired-trolling-law-is-waste-of-time-says-internet-campaigner-100252-30120150/
3 Trolling: Who does it and why? https://www.bbc.com/news/magazine-14898564

anyone who has had the misfortune of being trolled and abused on social media knows how futile and unsupportive these are reporting mechanisms can be. Automated replies that are vague and of no consequences. Trolls know very well how to subvert the terms of service and community standards to manipulate and avoid the automated moderation of social media channels. Police forces are ill-equipped, underfunded and just generally ignorant of online networks and social media sites and also unfamiliar with the law and legislation such as the Malicious Communications Act 1988. It also seemed at first sight very petty for someone to have to go to the police to report what someone was saying about them on social media. It can seem an insignificant and low priority to warrant police investigations into a Tweet. Yet, in many circumstances, the people at the receiving end of online and social media trolling and abuse do have valid complaints. We need to take online trolling seriously when it becomes threatening and abusive. This is because it can be said that super trolls have a lot in common with serial killers. Serial killers tend to demand attention, and that's something we can clearly see in the behaviour of trolls. They become obsessive and often come from turbulent backgrounds experiencing neglectful and abusive parents. Narcissism can fall into two distinctive categories. The grandiose who believe they indeed are tremendous and the vulnerable who overcompensate for their own perceived failures.

A study from a research team at the University of Winnipeg

in Canada revealed that trolls display the four characteristics of the "Dark Tetrad" [4]. The characteristics are psychopathy (an absence of empathy), narcissism (self-obsession), Machiavellianism (detached, calculating manipulativeness) and sadism (deriving pleasure from others' pain). The sadism element is all too prevalent when it comes to stories of trolling that have made the newspaper headlines. It seems all too common that one someone is grieving or that a tragic death has occurred, there are always an army of trolls ready and waiting to start shit posting on the memorial pages and or social media profiles of the persons who have died. To gain pleasure from upsetting already grieving family members, these trolls get a sadist kick of pleasure which puts them on par with psychopaths. There are multiple and almost endless amounts of stories like what follows.

- Family mourning loss of three members to Covid targeted by social media trolls [5].
- Sick trolls target grieving mum whose one-year-old daughter died suddenly in her sleep accusing her of 'sponging' off death with fundraising page [6].
- Caitlin Ruddy parents taunted by sick internet troll after daughter's tragic death [7].

4 Naming Evil: Dark Triad, Tetrad, Malignant Narcissism https://www.psychologytoday.com/intl/blog/beyond-heroes-and-villains/201606/naming-evil-dark-triad-tetrad-malignant-narcissism
5 https://www.theguardian.com/world/2020/nov/06/family-mourning-loss-of-three-members-to-covid-targeted-by-social-media-trolls-gladys-darren-dean-lewis-wales
6 https://www.thesun.ie/news/429122/sick-trolls-target-grieving-mum-whose-one-year-old-daughter-died-suddenly-in-her-sleep-accusing-her-of-sponging-off-death-with-fundraising-page/
7 https://www.chroniclelive.co.uk/news/north-east-news/caitlin-ruddy-parents-taunt-

• Grieving dad slammed Facebook after 'sick sadist' trolled him about his dead daughter [8].

I feel as if I could fill this entire book with headlines just like this. Trolling is at a level that is quite frightening if we then consider how many people are showing the serial killer traits of narcissism and sadism. Using social media to vent their wrath and take pleasure from upsetting other people. Trolling has become so toxic that it can even make people feel like they want to end their own lives. Again I can list multiple headlines of stories that fit this profile.

• A 14-Year-Old Girl's Suicide Is The Latest Front In The UK's Battle With Online Trolls[9].

• Charlotte Dawson commits suicide following extreme trolling[10].

• Family says online trolls drove young mom to suicide[11].

• 'Can you kill yourself already?' The vile online messages from internet trolls 'that led girl, 16, to hang herself'[12].

---

ed-sick-10758577

8 https://www.foxnews.com/tech/grieving-dad-slammed-facebook-after-sick-sadist-trolled-him-about-his-dead-daughter

9 https://www.businessinsider.com/hannah-smiths-suicide-and-online-trolls-2013-8

10 https://www.cosmopolitan.com/uk/reports/a25443/charlotte-dawson-dead-suicide-trolling/

11 https://nypost.com/2017/09/04/family-blames-online-trolls-for-driving-young-mom-to-suicide/

12 https://www.dailymail.co.uk/news/article-2246896/Jessica-Laney-16-committed-suicide-internet-trolls-taunted-told-kill-herself.html

I could go on and on and on. These examples are almost now infinite. There are hundreds if not thousands of dead as a result of social media trolling.

If you are a victim of online and social media trolling, you can take steps to protect yourself. You will find many good examples of advice online; you don't need me to explain it here. All I will say is the very best solution to online trolling is just to walk away from your social media. Lock it down, shut it down, delete it - whatever you have to do, just take a break from it. Someone's words can't hurt you anymore if you don't read them. And while it shouldn't be that you have to leave social media because of someone else's actions, it isn't necessarily a bad thing in long to think about quitting social media for good. At least to not use it on a regular daily basis. You will, in the long run, feel much better for it.

Trolling will always remain an issue. And there is a fine line between making fun and pulling someone's leg, then there is a sadist evil campaign of harassment against them. While social media companies will claim they are doing all they can to protect their users, angry people click more will always ensure that WRATH is allowed to fester and grow in strengthening our social networks.

Social Media And The Seven Deadly Sins

Rory Wilmer

Envy

"Resentment is like drinking poison and waiting for the other person to die. "
—— Carrie Fisher

THE GRASS IS ALWAYS GREENER

WE WANT YOU to be envious. In advertising one of the keys to changing your behaviour is making you subconsciously want something no matter if you need it or not. We need you to consume more. To buy more. To "lather, rinse and repeat". Social media is the ideal format and medium to stir up the sin of envy within us all. As we are already wired for our next dopamine hit of engagement we have been primed and set on shopping standby mode. Ready to add the next item to our virtual shopping baskets. To one click check out and wait for a courier to arrive in day or two with our shiny new goods. We didn't even have to take our assess off of our sofa. The goods just fall directly into our laps. It's with such ease that we are envious for more.

Our original sin of LUST helps drive our envious ways. As the first chapter in this book we looked at how social media taps into our sexual desires and provokes our feelings our lust engaging with our primal urges to procreate and indulge in our sexual fantasies. And its just our desire to have sex with someone or something that amplifies our sense of envy.

If you have ever looked at Facebook or Instagram and felt envious of someone else, you are not alone. The term 'social media envy' is real and it describes a situation which is linked to depression. In constantly viewing your social media feeds you are bombarded with a feed of content about other people's friends, family, accomplishments, travels and what can sometimes seem like their 'perfect lives'. This feed of content will at some point make you envious. You've probably felt this most recently during COVID-19 lockdowns. I know I have. While you work from home and dare not even leave your front door you see others sharing travel and holiday snaps from beachside resorts in Dubai. It makes you feel envious. You are stuck in a land locked city and can't even go to a bar or a cafe let alone go for a sunset walk along the beach with the sand in your feet and a cold beer in your hand. You feel depressed. You don't know when you will be able to go and see your parents again or where and when you go on a much deserved and needed vacation to the seaside resort you so dream of. In your envy you start to feel resentment and jealousy towards your friends as well as a sense of desperation and sadness within your self. Envy is a very poisonous and dangerous emotion to foster and social media amplifies and even creates this feeling within our selves.

A way to deal with this feeling is just always remind yourself that what you see on social media, is staged and curated. This envious life or situation you may be yearning for is not reality. The five star beach resort poolside photos don't reflect the Niagara falls style diarrhoea suffered from eating at the hotel buffet. The great night out party photos don't show the hangover from hell the next day as you wake in a pool of your own vomit in a bed of a complete stranger. There are always two sides to a story and only ever one side is shown on social media.

As we have worked our way through Social Media And The Seven Deadly Sins we can probably find elements of envy in all sins. Envy is a core driver for social media to work in the way it does. To motivate people to share content which is often so personal and intimate about them selves, as way of priming and peacocking their lives against others. The look at me attitude has only been personified by the advertising industry, which fawns over so-called influencers and social media celebrities as a vehicle to drive envy among users to push and pull them towards their products and brands.

In this chapter of ENVY I wondered what would best showcase examples on envy. Jealously is such a powerful and destructive emotion and it can be found at the root of all envious emotions towards others. Should I look for examples of where jealously has driven people to do fucked up things on social media? Well, I have already shown examples of that within each and every other chapter. I will showcase a few more examples, of course but what really should be the takeaway from this chapter is that there are ways to manage and handle your envy towards others and towards the provocation of constant consumerism.

Gratitude is an emotion which is best suited to battling your feelings of envy. Be grateful and thankful for what you have got. It is even suggested by research at Columbia University that feelings of gratitude and how you express them can actually and observably improve your health [1]. To improving your immune system, your sleeping patterns and also helping to reduce depression and anxiety. Gratitude is the ultimate virtue to counter envy [2]. The more we feel grateful for what we have the less envious we feel towards things that we don't have. It seems to simple to be true.

The period of lockdowns and curfews through this pandemic of COVID-19 has made feel more gratitude for what I have than ever before in my life. Home office has given me the opportunity to spend more quality time with my family. To share a desk with my stepsons as they do their remote school lessons while I participate in video conference calls to Los Angeles or New York.

The more locked-down and restricted we became the more grateful I felt for our apartment, its terrace and small garden. Gratitude that I could still do a job from home and work anywhere in the world remotely for a wide range of clients and brands. I felt humbled. I started to read more books. Time wasted commuting and feeling drained from the daily rat race of ferrying yourself across town traffic and into an office where a good proportion of the day and time was wasted anyway by constant distractions and trips to the coffee machine or water cooler where no longer being wasted. I could use an extra hour a day to read which in turn lead me to write more. And I feel so much gratitude for this

1 Gratitude Is a Boost to Health https://www.cuimc.columbia.edu/news/gratitude-boost-health
2 Expanding the Science and Practice of Gratitude https://ggsc.berkeley.edu/what_we_do/major_initiatives/expanding_gratitude

as it lead me to this point where I am finding myself writing the last chapters of a book which I felt I always to write but would always find some reason or excuse not to do it. I was envious of people who would and could write and found the time. Yet the moment I stayed to feel gratitude for what have was exactly when I found I also have the time and the will to sit down and write down my thoughts, feelings and observations after 2 years working in social media and global digital marketing.

As this is my first book I am sure that it is full of mistakes and things I could have done better. Yet I have to make these mistakes in order to understand and feel gratitude for what I have and how I can improve on the next edition, version or update of this book. And of course, I am envious of writers who can nail it in the second draft after a few days of writing and editing.

* * * * * *

AN EXAMPLE OF SOCIAL MEDIA ENVY

THE GREEN-EYED monster lurks around social media like a date rapist in a nightclub looking for the next drink to spike. Envy through social media is destroying natural beauty and nature. Instagram is the cause of this destruction. When a location or beauty spot becomes popular through the photographs of "influencers", hundreds if not thousands of other people head to that spot to recreate the image. To be the first of their friends to share an inspirational photo to let everyone know how adventurous, beautiful and talented they are. There are many examples of this, and here I list some of the articles written about the disturbing phenomenon.

- 15 destinations Instagram has helped ruin [1].
- Seven scenic spots being ruined by Instagram tourists, from Paris to Hong Kong [2].
- From poppy fields to Icelandic canyons, all the tourist destinations ruined by Instagram this year [3].

People are willing to trample down nature while trash and ruin surround their feet to make a photograph to impress others. This level of selfishness and herd mentality is driven by ENVY. The envious follow the envious searching for the next Instagram

1 https://www.insider.com/travel-destinations-instagram-influencers-ruined-2019-7
2 https://www.scmp.com/lifestyle/travel-leisure/article/3029938/seven-scenic-spots-being-ru-ined-instagram-tourists-paris
3 https://qz.com/quartzy/1580867/all-the-tourist-destinations-ruined-by-instagram-this-year/

photo, which can gain them hundreds of new followers and thousands of likes.

Moya Sarner writing in the Guardian spoke about Social Media envy in 2018 [4]. "We live in the age of envy. Career envy, kitchen envy, children envy, food envy, upper arm envy, holiday envy. You name it, there's an envy for it. Human beings have always felt what Aristotle defined in the fourth century BC as pain at the sight of another's good fortune, stirred by "those who have what we ought to have" [5] – though it would be another thousand years before it would make it on to Pope Gregory's list of the seven deadly sins." Moya claimed that social media had created a world in which everyone seems ecstatic. This was right and nearly four years on from these insights our envy only grows stronger as our usage of social media gets bigger.

In-depth studies have been undertaken to pinpoint precisely what triggers envy through our use of social media. A survey by Ruoyun Lin, Niels van de Ven and Sonja Utzac looked at the triggers. The abstract of their study reads as follows.

"Social network users often see their online friends post about experiential purchases (such as traveling experiences) and material purchases (such as newly purchased gadgets). Three studies (total N=798) were conducted to investigate which type of purchase triggers more envy on Social Network Sites (SNSs) and explored its underlying mechanism. We consistently

4 The age of envy: how to be happy when everyone else's life looks perfect https://www.theguardian.com/lifeandstyle/2018/oct/09/age-envy-be-happy-everyone-else-perfect-social-media
5 Rhetoric By Aristotle http://classics.mit.edu/Aristotle/rhetoric.mb.txt

found that experiential purchases triggered more envy than material purchases did. This effect existed when people looked at instances at their own Facebook News Feeds (Study 1), in a controlled scenario experiment (Study 2), and in a general survey (Study 3). Study 1 and 2 confirmed that experiential purchases increased envy because they were more self-relevant than material purchases. In addition, we found (in Study 1 and 3) that people shared their experiential purchases more frequently than material purchases on Facebook. So why do people often share experiential purchases that are likely to elicit envy in others? One answer provided in Study 3 is that people actually think that material purchases will trigger more envy. This paper provides insight into how browsing SNSs can lead to envy. It contributes to the research on experiential vs. material purchases and the emotion of envy [6]."

The more we use social media, the more we want to purchase things and share these purchases within our social networks. The more we share our purchases, including experiences, to our social networks, the more envy we create amongst our followers and friends. This, in turn, makes our followers and friends make more purchases and have more experiences which we then see and ourselves and once again become envious. The vicious cycle continues. This is all, of course, music to the advertiser's ears and what all consumerists and capitalists want to hear. The more we

---

6 What triggers envy on Social Network Sites? A comparison between shared experiential and material purchases https://www.sciencedirect.com/science/article/pii/S0747563218301547

share, the more we buy! Perfect. Make them all envious of one another, so they never stop buying.

You have probably experienced this on more than one occasion. You talk about a topic or some product, and the very next time you check your social media feeds, you are served an advert for that very same product. While social media companies swear blind that they are not listening to your conversation, it can be proven that they have been doing just that in some circumstances. Facebook admitted that it was listening to private conversations after investigations and many hundreds of articles by investigative journalists, which felt and hunch this unethical practice was taking place[7]. The headlines made for good reading, but as within all headlines, the reality was much less sensational than the clickbait would have you believe.

"In early August 2019, Bloomberg News published a story revealing how Facebook had contracted an external company to transcribe audio conversations conducted through the Facebook Messenger app. The process was engaged to test the accuracy of an automatic transcription algorithm Facebook was rolling out, and the company claimed all users who opted in to the transcription service were aware of the potential human review system. While some reports questioned how transparent Facebook's notification process actually was, the story rapidly spread across media outlets, with a vast of array of headlines

---

7 Facebook admits it was listening to your private conversations, too https://www.digitaltrends.com/news/facebook-admits-it-was-also-listening-to-your-private-conversations/

dramatically affirming, Facebook admits it was listening to your private conversations [8]."

So it sticks in most people's minds that Facebook and Instagram are listening to us. And we laugh it off and joke about it. It becomes just accepted that we are being spied upon in this era of Surveillance Capitalism. A disturbing indication of how far this system has infected our minds and made us subservient to their penetration into our minds. However, Instagram and Facebook ads aren't listening to your conversations to know what product to sell you next. It is just a coincidence that you talk about something and then you see an advert for it. Well, more than coincidence, it is the raw and tangible illustration of the power of social media prediction algorithms. Social networks know us better than we know ourselves. They know what we want before we want it or just when we start our consumer journey to purchase it. The algorithm has been fed with some data signals, and of all of the data exhaust we leave behind both on and off social media sites, it knows exactly when is the right moment and the right product to feed us with. If it hadn't have been for our envy and all of our other Seven Deadly Sins, the algorithm wouldn't have got as powerful and all-seeing as it is today. We fed the Eye of Sauron until it bled and puked the data signals back at us at such speed and ferocity that we could do nothing but surrender and submit to its BUY NOW CLICK HERE messages.

---

8 Facebook isn't secretly listening to your conversations, but the truth is much more disturbing
https://newatlas.com/computers/facebook-not-secretly-listening-conversations/

We have to break our social media habits to stop this vice of ENVY. To be grateful for what we have got. To prevent our envy of others. To not allow the feelings of wanting or needing more as a way to impress others or gain likes and engagements from our social networks. For as long as we are fostering and harbouring envy, we will forever be stuck in the grip of the social media cycle of always wanting more. It is time for a mass intervention into our addiction.

We may drive a great big Cadillac. So in the words of William DeVaughn. Be thankful for what you got. It's time to quit this bad habit and reclaim our lives and minds for a better future for humanity.

Rory Wilmer

Chapter 11

Pride

"A proud man is always looking down on things and people; and, of course, as long as you are looking down, you cannot see something that is above you."

— C.S. Lewis, Mere Christianity

PRIDE AND PREJUDICE

WRATH HAS BROUGHT us here. Combined with every other sin. Our pride is what keeps us coming back to social media. Our addiction feeds our pride and ensures we cannot switch off or put down our mobile phones. One more look at the news feed. Let me just check what the red dot notification is about. How many likes has my last post gained? How many views did my latest story receive? My pride won't let me stop. It's 3am, and I can't sleep, yet I still want to swipe open my phone and look at my news feed. Did someone post something interesting from a night out with friends, and I wasn't invited to join them? When you finally get to sleep, you soon wake up, and the first thing you do is reach for your phone. You unlock it, and you start looking at your social media. You are checking your feed before you have even gone to the toilet, or in most cases, you are using the bathroom as you check your social media [1]. If this is you. You have a problem, and you need to start a digital detox immediately.

I feel I was one of the last lucky generations to grow up in a time where we weren't always on stage in front of an audience. Millennials and Generation Z are born into a world where they appear on social media even without their consent as their parents post newborn baby pictures direct from the hospital maternity wards. Some are even live-streamed into this

---

[1] MORE THAN HALF OF FACEBOOK USERS USE IT WHILE ON THE TOILET https://www.valuewalk.com/2015/09/use-facebook-on-the-toilet/

world as parents broadcast the births of their children in real-time. There is constant pressure to use social media to make sure you are visible on the network to validate your existence. I'm very relieved and pleased that my stepsons don't have any interest in social media. At ages 12 and 9, they show little to no care for mainstream social media and not even TikTok. They have WhatsApp, and their friends and peers seem to be highly active by the number of notifications. However, our boys just ignore their phones for days, if not even weeks. They simply don't care. They find it boring and not interesting. We are lucky to have a couple of kids who seem to be bucking the general trend. Our sons would rather play video games, read manga books, or watch anime or horror series. They are coming across as very social media savvy. They know it's something to use with care and caution and not something to waste their time on. This is the hope that Generation Alpha give us. They will be the generation that heads back to the moon and onwards to Mars. They have bigger and better things to do than waste their minds on social media. My wife and I didn't have to try and persuade our sons into this state of mind when it comes to avoiding social media. It's just something they have discovered for themself. For this, I am highly grateful. As I would say to anyone reading this book who has young children, don't let them use social media until they are well into their teens from 15 onwards. It may sound harsh and draconian but let me be clear, social media is not good or healthy for children. It should come with health warnings, and much like cigarettes and alcohol, it should be regulated and only allowed for people over the ages of 18 to consume. Yet, it is unlike that this will ever happen. If Mark Zuckerberg gets his way, he wants all of your children to use social media. On May 10th 2021, the National Association of Attorney's General wrote an open letter to Mark Zuckerberg. The signatures make it clear that creating a children's Instagram is a terrible idea in the letter.

"Research increasingly demonstrates that social media can be harmful to the physical, emotional, and mental well-being of children. In the last decade, increasing mental distress and treatment for mental health conditions among youth in North America has paralleled a steep rise in the use of smartphones and social media by children and adolescents. Research shows a link between young people's use of social media and the increase in mental distress, self-injurious behaviour and suicidality among youth. In fact, an online-monitoring company tracking the activity of 5.4 million children found that Instagram was frequently flagged for suicidal ideation, depression and body image concerns."

Research quoted in the letter suggests that "Instagram and social media are killing our children". Yet Mark Zuckerberg's pride means he will do anything to continue the growth hacking of his user base and that he won't and can't stop until he really does everyone on the planet signed up to his network. Our pride as users means we are unwilling to challenge it. Only learned colleagues, professionals of psychology and medical experts are sounding the alarm and making it very clear that Instagram for kids is a terrible idea and that children using social media in any form has harmful consequences. Yet this information, it seems, still doesn't feed through to most parents who allow their children to use mobile phones and social media unsupervised. Data from Statistica shows that nearly 6% of the entire user base of Facebook is between the age of 13-17.[2] And we will never really know the actual number of under 13-year-olds using the site as you are supposed to be 13 or over to use the site, so there is no way to log a younger age who can easily make a profile claiming to be any age they so wish. There are no checks or age verifications when you open a new account. You wouldn't let your children smoke. So why do you let them use social media?

* * * * * *

CHECK YOURSELF BEFORE YOU WRECK YOURSELF

PRIDE CAN DRIVE a lot of social media engagement and dictate how we respond to others. Yet mainly, it is caused by a desire to talk about ourselves. We use social media as a mask to project an image of ourselves in the way in which we want others to see us. So our PRIDE takes control. When something or someone comes along that challenges our beliefs or the image of ourselves that we have been busy curating and nurturing on social media, our pride is activated. And we go into the territory of social media wrath, as we have seen in the chapters previously. If someone on your friend's list suddenly challenges your content by pointing out a mistake, you have made or perhaps even an element of hypocrisy in what you post, you unfriend and ban them. You don't want people to challenge your narrative about yourself; you just wish to reinforce your PRIDE in what you are stating or projecting about yourself.

In recent years I have noticed a trend in which people have started to resent and be hateful towards people who have made self-made success. There is such a sense of social injustice against entrepreneurs, especially in the United Kingdom, where it seems that success is somehow a bad thing. Could this be the hangover curse of Labour Momentum, poisoning social media with its 'stop the global elite' rhetoric and constant bashing of self-made billionaires as if they and new money are the roots of all evil and the cause of all societies problems? People are cynical, and they lash out at other people's real-world success when it is so out of reach of their own achievements. They are all too willing and happy to post about their latest gains and achievements, but when the accomplishments of entrepreneurs and billionaires hit the news feeds, they must find a way to belittle it or knock it down.

A dyslexic teenager drops out of university and creates one of the most successful corporations in UK history, an empire including publishing, music production, airline travel, package holidays, train travel, telecoms and internet, healthcare and banking. He gets called a 'twat' for being successful.

A fellow starts a business in his garage, selling books through a website he made all by himself. He walks each day to the post office carrying packages to send out the orders. He works 18+ hours a day for the first few years to make it a success. His business becomes the most valuable business globally, selling everything to everyone and offering IT and Internet services to governments and corporations worldwide. He gets called a 'cunt' for being successful. At the age of 13, he wrote his first software. He went onto university but decided to drop out and form his own microcomputer company called Microsoft. He revolutionised home and office computing and created the world's biggest market for IT software and hardware. He becomes for some time the worlds richest man and sits firmly in the top ten richest men.

He donates a significant proportion of his money to charity and helps millions upon millions of people avoid the deadly disease. He gets called a child-killing satanist who wants to enslave the world with microchips.

He was born in Budapest while the Austro-Hungarian empire collapsed around him. Nationalism was on the rise, and soon, the goose-steps of the SS would be heard on his street. As a young 13-year-old Jewish boy, he knew very well what Nazism would mean for him and his family. Through cunningness and bravery, you survive the fight against fascism and move to London to study economics. London in 1947 wasn't the big party city that you can imagine of the hipsters of Shoreditch today. It was grim and brutal. You manage to study and work your way up to change your life from an immigrant Jew to a global financier. You become one of the richest men in the world, and then you decide you will give away your wealth to help others. As your experiences during the dark period of Nazism taught you that fascism should never be allowed to raise its ugly head again. You get called a cunt, twat, global elitist who wants to eat babies and take over the world to enslave humanity.

I have only used four examples of men here. I could and will continue this list to include successful women. Because the hatred thrown towards women in social media is far more significant and abusive than the hate thrown towards successful men.

Social Media has made you angry. It has made you wrathful. It has turned you into a cynic and prepared to abuse and accuse anyone and everyone who manages to be successful and create self-made wealth. Rather than concentrate on old family money and the ruling elites who have been in power since medieval times, you decide to attack modern wealth instead of the aristocratic and historical wealth of old money. That is where the true power and greed lies. In the old money. Not in the new capital. Yet, it is satisfying to call someone expletives on social media using slang terms assigned to female anatomy. It is easier to do this than to consider that if you tried a bit harder and had more of an entrepreneurial and hard-working spirit, perhaps you could have a little slice of the wealth distributed to those who work hard enough for it.

* * * * * *

THE POLITICS OF PRIDE

"OPINIONS ARE LIKE assholes; everybody's got one..." So said Simone Elkeles, and in today's social media-driven world, assholes have instantaneous opinions on multiple social media channels. The worst kind of assoholery can be found in political discourse on social media. In the past five years, it has been taken to new levels. In the west with the likes of Trump in the USA, in Brazil with Jair Bolsonaro and the general rise of right-wing populist politics all over Europe from Boris Joynson in the UK to Viktor Orbán in Hungary. The "left" is nowhere to be seen. Only the radical and extreme left that we saw in the chapter WRATH. Which are nothing more than Stalinist Marxists looking for their next violent revolution. Or so social media would have you believe.

Social Media has been hijacked by politics and by politicians and political parties. As social media is the perfect platform to divide and conquer. It is primed to create and amplify polarisation. To aid in syndicating rhetoric through an echo chamber of self-propelling virility and reproduction.

I've been asked many times to give talks and presentations to Central European political parties and politicians. I have been offered very handsome financial rewards for doing so. To work on political campaigns and to advise on social media tactics and strategies for elections. I have always refused to do so. I did for a short period no longer than six months, finding myself working for a political lobbyist. Yet, it didn't take me long to discover the kind of graft and illegality he was involved in for me to run away from it before it got out of hand. I was disgusted with myself that I let my vice of GREED get to me. I was offered distance riches and a leading creative role, yet it was a cover and smokescreen for orchestrating and vehicle to steal public money. I saw the dark side of political lobbying in that short time, and I decided that I would never again be tempted by the dark side. I saw how these dark forces lusted over social media and saw it as yet another tool in their toolbox for use to extort, manipulate, and control public and private opinions to extract leverage for use in lobbying activities and as political motivations engineer how people voted.

Having managed to get out of the situation with nothing more lost than my own PRIDE, I decided to get my head down and return to the safety of global brand advertising and focusing on becoming one of the leading strategists in my city. Politics was not for me. There was nothing more I despised than politicians. As much as I wanted to infiltrate their parties and bring them down from within, I just wouldn't have the stomach to be around for them for the amount of time required to achieve such an operation.

Politics and political rhetoric is rotting social media from within. It reminds me of a local pub with a sign on the door that said "No Politics, No Religion". The only two rules for entering the pub was to leave these two subjects outside. While many people like to discuss these two subjects over a drink or two, they inevitably always lead to a disagreement and even something more physical, and I don't mean a hug. We fight. We fight over politics and our political parties. Nowhere do we fight the most then in the virtual pubs of our time, social media.

Donald Trump has epitomized where we are at in terms of PRIDE and social media. His confrontational and self-obsessive style made him the textbook social media sociopath. Years before he stepped up to run as the Republican nominee for President, he had been using social media to lambast, taunt, bully and provoke others. No one really cared when he was merely Donald Trump, the real estate mogul and reality TV celebrity. That was all part of his persona. When he became the 45th president of the United States of America, then every tweet and social media post he would make would all each and every one of them become headline news. The media obsession with Twitter does more harm than it does good. Twitter is a tool for lazy journalists, and the majority of journalists are lazy. It spoons them statements and quotes that they can copy and paste into a narrative that best suits their news agenda. For the majority of Donald Trump's campaign and presidency, Twitter didn't mind this at all. Each night on the prime time news, you would hear the words TWITTER and TWEETED and TWEETS concerning the

President. Jack Dorsey, the founder of CEO of Twitter, loved that. He didn't care at that time that some of the tweets of the President were in direct contradiction and conflict with Twitters own "community standards" policies.

Social media predicted the win of Donald Trump over Hillary Clinton in 2016. The writing was on our social media walls. Social media data analysts worldwide were predicting success for Donald Trump based on the volume of social media mentions and positive sentiment that could be assigned to him through these mentions. Yet the traditional polls got it so wrong. Had social media now become a more accurate tool for predicting election victory? It would seem so.

"Analysts monitoring the social media activity of both campaigns on the major social media channels saw the outcome of this election coming months ago, and kept talking about the massive silent voter base that was forming around the Republican nominee. Social media analysts continually sounded the alarm that all of the polls were not reflecting the actual situation on the ground in the pre-election landscape," said Phil Ross, a social media analyst at Socialbakers.

Hillary Clinton had outspent Trump on TV advertising. Which was traditionally the fastest route to the Whitehouse. Yet, it didn't make much difference. In this day and age, if you don't win on social media, you are not, as Charlie Sheen would say, HASHTAG WINNING. Donald Trump managed to turn the wave of mentions into a spiral of positive sentiment that washed up within all the negative sentiment against him and turned it into self-deprecating memes. Love him or hate him, Donald Trump is the master of media manipulation. His mastery of dominating traditional media faired well on social media in an age of "political correctness gone mad" and the widespread resentment and disappointment in conventional politics and politicians to deliver change to the average Joe Bloggs and Jane Doe. Populism was popular again, and that was something very much to do with how social media has shaped us. In a world where we seek constant likes, shares, and comments to feed our addiction to engagement, we all seek our own form of self populism through our social media channels. So when a populist politician turns up using the language of the everyday man and referencing openly well-known internet MEME and conspiracy theories, they are going to capture the attention of hundreds of millions of people. The staggering amount of social media junkies who are primed to follow the call of such a pied piper of populist thinking and rhetoric. In any other political reality, an Access Hollywood tape of the candidate saying he "grabbed women by the pussy" would be enough to end their political career. Yet for Trump, this only endorsed him more to the locker room type of mentality but not only that, it just reinforced his position to his already loyal and growing base of women! It is unfathomable to imagine who in the #METOO age such a statement can make you more popular, not less. Trump being Trump, did what he did best; he turned the Access Hollywood tape into a conspiracy theory by suggesting it was 'fake'. As he would go on to describe as fake all the sexual assault allegations against him that stetted to surface as a result of his electioneering.

Many women came forward to talk of how Trump had groped them or pushed himself onto them. There were videos of Trump dancing the night away with the sexual predator and alleged paedophile Jeffrey Epstein. In the video, Trump makes obviously sexually related comments about the young female guests at a young model's party. Ex playboy models [1] and porn stars would also come forward to share their experiences of Trump's sexual affairs while he was married to Melina - cumulating in the Stormy Daniels pay off [2]. Trump had used his personal Lawyer Michael Cohen to make a hush-money payment to Stormy to ensure she spills the beans about their affair. That didn't work, and the story became global news as the fallout made its way through the media circus and then into the courts. All of this was not enough to stop Trump from winning the election. The PRIDE of social media had been enough to ensure that he would win and win big. Even if he did get a little help from his friends in Moscow.

For a long time, the Russian's have known that subversion is their most significant asset when facing a threat in which they

1 Former 'Playboy' Model Spills Details Of Alleged Affair: Trump 'Tried To Pay Me' https://www.npr.org/sections/thetwo-way/2018/03/23/596257288/former-playboy-model-spills-alleged-affair-details-trump-tried-to-pay-her
2 Trump Admits To Authorizing Stormy Daniels Payoff, Denies Sexual Encounter https://www.npr.org/2018/05/02/607943366/giuliani-says-trump-did-know-about-stormy-daniels-payment?t=1629618226005

can't beat in a head-on military confrontation. They use leverage where they have it. The Russians have leverage through their psychological warfare and their ability to harness the power of social media to manipulate an entire electorate into helping them achieve the political outcomes they perceive as being in their favour. While the Russians have been in the lead in this kind of subversion, the Chinese have soon caught up, and just by the nature of the internet and social media, even nations like Iran and North Korea can step and pay to play. The Trump election success of 2016 is probably the most high profile social media success of Russian subversion in modern times [3]. Yet close behind it is BREXIT [4].

It's within Russians interests that the EU is weakened. There was no greater political event since the creation of the EU to weaken it than BREXIT. The UK's decision to leave the trading block will have repercussions for decades to come, and it was a crucial strike against the unity of Europe and NATO. One of the main reasons for the voting success, social media. At the centre of this, all is Facebook and the Cambridge Analytics scandal. While Cambridge Analytica denied working for any BREXIT campaigns, it soon became apparent that in fact, they did [5]. We are also well aware of Dominic Cummings and Vote Leave and their passion for data driven messaging based on social media

3 RUSSIANACTIVEMEASURESCAMPAIGNSANDINTERFERENCE INTHE2016U.S.ELECTION
https://www.intelligence.senate.gov/sites/default/files/documents/Report_Volume1.pdf
4 U.K. Probes Russian Social Media Influence in Brexit Vote https://www.bloomberg.com/news/articles/2017-11-02/u-k-probes-russian-social-media-influence-in-brexit-vote
5 Cambridge Analytica did work for Brexit groups, says ex-staffer https://www.politico.eu/article/cambridge-analytica-leave-eu-ukip-brexit-facebook/

insights [6]. Our addiction to social media, combined with our venerability to our vice of PRIDE, created the perfect system and methods for tipping the balance of elections into your favour to whoever had the most relevant data. This data was quite often gathered illegally and most definitely used unethically.

To win elections, you don't need to persuade millions of people to vote for you. You need to micro-target the undecideds and fence-sitters to swing them towards your position. There was no better way to get people's attention and hijack the conversation than by using social media ads designed to trigger your sense of pride by knowing exact psychographics, demographic, and geographic data about you. Angry people click more, and the more enraged I can make you through my Facebook posts, the more likely you will be to click on a link that leads you down a sales funnel. Yet this isn't an e-commerce sales funnel, and the checkout is making you put a tick in a box on a voting slip and not entering your credit card details, and pushing buy now. Yet, it's still the same funnel and with the same methodology and outcomes. A conversion rate.

To anyone who has been on social media these past five years, you will be more than aware of what I am talking about. We have all been subjected to a tsunami of politicised social media content. Endless posts about BREXIT. Constant fights about "right" and "left". The infinite stream of age-old polarised arguing

6 Brexit ad blitz data firm paid by Vote Leave broke privacy laws, watchdogs find https://techcrunch.com/2019/11/27/brexit-ad-blitz-data-firm-paid-by-vote-leave-broke-privacy-laws-watchdogs-find/

that Conservatives hate the poor and the Marxists radicalism that poor should eat the rich. Where this is most profound is on Facebook. From once being a network where friends could connect and share photos with each other, it has become a politicised platform that is nothing more than the world's most significant classified ads page. Yet, these classified ads are not put into easily searchable sections where you know how to find what you are looking for. These ads are targeted directly to you based on your innermost secrets and behaviours. Designed to trigger your cognitive biases in ways you won't even know how or why. The technical way adverts have been designed to make you want and buy things has now been taken over by the politicians and political groups who want you to help put them into power. So they can enjoy the ill-gotten gains of political power and all the graft and financial benefits and paybacks which come with it. As we are the addicts of social media, we only care about our next hit. We don't care how the cartels supply and import our hits; we only care if the local dealer has enough of what we want to supply our needs at that time. Each and every time I log into social media, my addiction is served. If I allow all the notifications to stay active, my hits are supplied even when I am not on the channel. Social media is the cartel and the dealer at the same time.

Unless we wean ourselves away from social media, or at least demand change, politicians and political parties and foreign threat actors are going to take advantage of collective junkie state of mind. Social media should not be politicised. Social media companies should not have political lobbyists on their payroll. Social media should not take political campaigning advertising money. This is because it is proven that social media can manipulate and change the course of democracy, and it is not accountable for its actions, whatever the end result may be.

In 2021 during the midterm elections in the US, I VOTED stickers started appearing on the Facebook network. Facebook had offered users the option to display this sticker on their profile. It would indicate to their friends and family and the wider public that they had been out and cast their vote. This 'harmless' sticker turned out to be an experiment run by Facebook to see if they could get more people to vote by using peer pressure and the cognitive bias of social proof [7].

"It turns out that people were a little more likely to vote — and definitely more likely to tell Facebook they'd voted — if they saw their friends had voted too. Eighteen percent of people who didn't see a list of friends who'd voted clicked on the "I Voted" sticker; 20 percent of people who did see the list of friends clicked on it. And users who saw both the sticker and the list of friends were slightly more likely (about 0.6 percent) to actually go to the polls than users who didn't see anything."

This is precisely the kind of social proof and peer pressure

7 Facebook's "I Voted" sticker was a secret experiment on its users https://www.vox.com/2014/11/4/7154641/midterm-elections-2014-voted-facebook-friends-vote-polls

influence we seek in corporate advertising and branding. We know there is nothing more powerful than a recommendation from a friend, and word of mouth has the power to influence more than anything else. And what is social media if it isn't just one big platform for word of mouth. So Facebook, as their own experiments show, have the power to influence elections. Sometimes it is in their control, often it is not. How did we allow a social media site created for college students to hook up to become one of the most significant and deciding factors for democracy?

* * * * * *

FROM THE ARAB SPRING TO MASS MURDER IN MYANMAR

WHEN ENOUGH PEOPLE gather en masse in a town square or a piazza, they can start a revolution. From the Czechoslovakian student marches of 1989 on Prague's Wenceslas Square to the Chinese students who gathered on Tiananmen Square. These gatherings can create events that reverberate throughout time and space and have political and social consequences that last for decades to come. Yet what happens with people gather in the public and town square spaces of social media? Can social media bring enough people together to form a momentum of a group that can incite revolution?

The Arab Spring was a revolutionary wave that spread through the Middle East and Northern Africa in 2021 and 2012.

The role social media played during the Arab spring is debatable as many uprisings occurred throughout the region regardless of usage of internet [1]. However, social media did play a role in organising and massing large groups of people out onto the streets in protest. These protests weren't exclusive to anti-government protestors, either. Social media played a part for both sides in the fight between pro-democracy demonstrators and the government loyalists and their supporters. In Egypt, they went that extra step and even cut off access to the Internet to stop the spread and momentum of the Arab Spring movement.

---

1 Social Media and the Arab Spring: Politics Comes First https://journals.sagepub.com/doi/pdf/10.1177/1940161212471716

If in doubt, pull out the plug. "Have you tried turning it off and on again".

The roots of the social media activity within the timeline of the Arab spring have been traced back to the Tunisian revolution. After this event young Egyptian's spread the call to protest online with the help of a Facebook campaign, "We Are All Khaled Said," organised by the April 6 Youth Movement, Egypt's "largest and most active online human-right activist group [2]." As the online anger grew and the sentiment spread to reach many within metropolitan and urban areas, they were driven out to the streets through the mechanism of Facebook events. A type of post where you can organise an event, add a date, time and a place and allow people to sign up if they are interest or going. This action shares it with their friends, creating a large and significant reach for events that get a few thousand people to indicate interest. A few thousand people clicking they are interested in an event is enough for the event itself to reach over a million people. An event post contains its own mini content timeline so the events can be updated in real-time with important information and as many MEME as your photoshop designer can create.

If you are old enough, you are familiar with the colour-coded revolutions of the cold war and early 90s. From the success of the velvet revolution to the failure of the Orange revolutions, European revolutions have been ever so colourful. A rainbow

---

2 Harlow, Summer (2013). "It Was a "Facebook Revolution": Exploring the Meme-Like Spread of Narratives During the Egyptian Protests". Revista De Communicacion. 12: 59–82.

of revolution freeing people from the Tyrannies of the relics of soviet Marxist- Lenin totalitarian socialism. As we moved into the age of social media, this would become the new colour of choice. A transparent colour that could cross all borders and start chain reactions across multiple states and regimes that would destabilise and, in some cases, topple regimes and governments favouring the West's supporters and our capitalist consumer democracy branded style of freedom. Social media was now one of the main theatres of war and one of the many new digital battlegrounds that all sides had to partake in and fight for the attention of humanity as we scrolled further and further down our timelines. We were not even taking our eyes off of our mobile phones as the world around us burned.

This new war in the "metaverse [3]" was always going to get bloody. It wouldn't just stay as a MEME and a harmless post on a website invented by a handful of introvert nerds in California. This was now a tool of states, a weapon of armies and a means of espionage and psychological warfare. Facebook, and not for the first time in its history, ended up with blood on its hands [4]. Facebook has admitted it failed to prevent its platform from being used by the Military in Myanmar to incite genocide [5]. Yes, you read that correctly. Facebook posts have the power to

---

3 What is the metaverse? https://theconversation.com/what-is-the-metaverse-2-media-and-information-experts-explain-165731
4 Facebook Admits It Was Used to Incite Violence in Myanmar https://www.nytimes.com/2018/11/06/technology/myanmar-facebook.html
5 An Independent Assessment of the Human Rights Impact of Facebook in Myanmar https://about.fb.com/news/2018/11/myanmar-hria/

provoke and enact genocide [6].

While Facebook insists that they "stand against hate and violence" one can only conclude that they are somewhat responsible for the world's increased amount of hate and violence in our world today [7]. Our PRIDE has been so manipulated by our addiction to social media that we constantly find ourselves in confrontations with one another. Be they political, spiritual and psychical, our senses have been hijacked by our addiction to social media engagement. Information overload makes you angry and social media is information overload on steroids [8]. Angry people click more, which aids in the revenue streams for Facebook and all other social networks to serve more adverts and charge more fees for outbound clicks while impressing their media agencies and advertisers with ever-increasing click through and engagement rates. Sadness spreads quicker than joy. It is a proven fact. Anger is viral much faster than humour. Rage is the emotion to spread the quickest on social media [9]. And rage often stems from our pride.

We have to look back through all our vices at the seven deadly sins and see how each and every one of them has been harnessed in a way to keep us online, engaged with and addicted to social media. Until we start to release our attention has been

6 A Genocide Incited on Facebook, With Posts From Myanmar's Military https://www.nytimes.com/2018/10/15/technology/myanmar-facebook-genocide.html
7 Online hate increasing against minorities, says expert https://www.ohchr.org/EN/NewsEvents/Pages/sr-minorities-report.aspx
8 Information Overload: Why Social Media Makes Us Angry https://medium.com/@awryleigh/information-overload-why-social-media-makes-us-angry-3e5d66cd02d
9 What Emotion Goes Viral the Fastest? https://www.smithsonianmag.com/science-nature/what-emotion-goes-viral-fastest-180950182/

hijacked and that social media addiction is a real and present danger, we will continue to live in a world where one post on Facebook can start a genocide.

Rory Wilmer

III. ALL YOUR BASE ARE BELONG TO US.

Rory Wilmer

Chapter 12

The Seven Virtues

"It is not always the same thing to be a good man and a good citizen." —— Aristotle, Selected Writings From The Nicomachean Ethics And Politics.

SEVEN VIRTUES

SOCIAL MEDIA AND the internet at large is not all the complete shit show which I may have portrayed it to be in this book. Our sinful behaviour through the manipulation of our core vices are what fuel the vast majority of social media engagements and addiction. However I want to acknowledge that there is also another-side. Humanity as the ability to show great kindness to one another, to be incredibly creative and inspiring and also to have a great feeling and acknowledgement that we are one and part of nature and the symbiotic infrastructure of planet earth. Our species craves for interaction with one another, we are a social species. We thrive in groups and through our connections to one another. Our languages, our creativity our music all of which can cross cultures and link us as one being together.

There are many random acts of kindness that happen and many happen through online communities and social media actions. Social media has a great potential to do good for humanity by allowing us a global village connection to one an all no matter where they are on this planet. For each and ever vice there is a virtue and for each and ever vice I could list and find examples of where people have done amazing things for one another through the internet and by using social media. That in its self could be an entirely stand alone book.

For each and every vice there is a virtue. Please take a

moment to consider these seven virtues and how you can utilise them in your daily life and through you social media channels.

- Chastity
- Temperance
- Charity
- Diligence
- Patience
- Kindness
- Humility

Social Media And The Seven Deadly Sins

Rory Wilmer

Chapter 13

A post Facebook world

"All good things must come to an end, but all bad things can continue forever."
— Thornton Wilder

WHAT'S NEXT FOR SOCIAL MEDIA?

THE SOCIAL MEDIA landscape is changing. As Facebook starts to loose popularity and heads down the same curve as sites like MySpace did, services such as TikTok step up to take the crown away from Zuckerberg and co [1]. While Facebook Inc has desperately tried to buy and copy its way out of its inventible decline, the writing so to speak is on the wall or do we we say news feed these days? The banning and de-platforming of Donald Trump signals the beginning of the end for sites like Facebook and Twitter. Who for too long have held too much of our attention and addicted us to their networks so they could gain great wealth from the colossal advertising budgets that big brands are willing to invest to get just a few seconds of our attention. With our short attention spans the format of short format video is here to stay.

ByteDance, the Chinese company behind TikTok have penetrated so deeply within the social media addicts that they are now reaping the financial, and data rewards that come with it. Soon China will have a full window not only into the entire world though the app, but a window into everyone's soul through the psychographics data they can harvest from their app. Something we all should be somewhat wary of yet the majority wont care. They are happy to pay their price of selling their soul for he return

1 [1] TikTok is the new Facebook – and it is shaping the future of tech in its image https://www.the-guardian.com/commentisfree/2021/aug/16/tiktok-facebook-tech-future-chinese-video-app

of engagements on their karaoke videos.

As Facebook becomes the preferred social network for your grandparents and parents, the youth move towards the new as quickly as the sun sets into the ocean. My own kids call Facebook and Instagram "cringe" and thankfully they are not interested in it all. They have gone back into the IRC style chatrooms that is Discord where they talk in voice and text chat with their friends and play games together in realtime on Roblox and PlayStation. This makes me so happy, that this Generation Alpha sees through the stupidity and waste of time that social media has become. For the rest of us, Social media should and will become more focused on smaller groups, on real communities and more about local events and neighbourhoods as opposed to the global village.

There are now many competitors and new social media networks on competition to the monsters of Twitter, Facebook and Instagram. All with different models of business and or niche community outlooks. I could start to name them here but as social media and the industry changes and moves so fast, as soon as I publish this book there is a chance that these sites are shut down, or they have been floated on the stock market or bought out for billions of dollars by Mark Zuckerberg. The point I am making is that there are alternatives to the main social networks, but they still always have the same methods and tactics as their root. They want you the user to spend as much time as possible on site and in app.

My advice is to limit your social media to a couple of networks that actually have a benefit to you. To check them as infrequently as you can. Start at once a day and then work your way down to once a week. The time you gain back in your life will improve your health and allow you to focus again on what matters most.

Chapter 14

Logging off

LOG OFF

THE EASIEST WAY to detox from social media is to delete the apps from your phone. It sounds easier to do that it really is. I managed to do it and what I found was both frightening but also rewarding.

When you delete social media apps from your phone it takes some time for your psychical body to stop trying to open them up again. You are so used to opening these apps multiple times each day that you have created muscle memory in your arms, hands and fingers. You will automatically swipe your phone to the page where your social media app icons were place and your thumb will involuntarily push down as if the app icon is still there. This should be enough to tell you that you had a problem. Take action today.

Log off.
Uninstall.

SM&7DS THE SHOW

AS I WAS WRITING this book, a colleague reached out to me to say they were interested in my writing. As we discussed this book and the project more, it became clear that there was a powerful concept for a drama series within it. The Seven Deadly Sins of Social Media are something we can all relate to. We have all had experiences of at least one if not more or all of them at some point during our time being the rats in the experimental test tube of social media life. I felt that these are stories that need to be told to a broader audience. To try and show people that social media can be a destructive force in their lives. That they and they alone have the power to take back control of their lives and overcome their addictions to social media.

With this in mind, I set about writing a seven-part series anthology show. Each episode explored the darker side of social media and told stories around the behaviour of original sins that social media extracts from all of us. The project soon took off, and I soon found myself on calls to Hollywood and enlisting a talented British screenwriter to the project. Matt worked in Hollywood as a writer for over twenty years. He specialised in crime and history, having recently been a writer for Oliver Stone's The Untold History of the United States.

It was surreal to go from an idea of a book to suddenly being a part of the writing room. We were about to develop one of the most exciting and essential TV shows about new technology and its relationship to humanity since Black Mirror while also being an anthology as terrifying and iconic as something like the Outer Limits. That was a daunting and yet exhilarating feeling.

"At the end of the twentieth century, the human race developed a new technology which allowed humanity to perfectly externalize and communicate its emotions, driven by the science of computers. Social Media allowed the entire human race to communicate with itself as one - a technological utopia that symbolized man's triumph over adversity. There was a design flaw that no one anticipated: this process had an unexpected side effect which no one foresaw - it accidentally tapped into humanity's dark side, and allowed this darkness to spill unrestricted into this giant online consciousness, polluting it. Facebook, the symbol of this new utopia and the showpiece consumer technology of the age, became a gigantic mainframe for the dark side of humanity, responsible for dividing the human race instead of uniting it. The root of this darkness is human desire itself - powerful, and addicting - and it affects everyone who uses social media, because everyone has that desire within them.

This is a series about that darkness and how its true and terrifying power is to turn users into addicts of the very technology that was supposed to liberate them - a hideous nightmare version of the utopia its founders intended. Technology was supposed to liberate us, but in the process - it ended up imprisoning us. This is an anthology series of stories which will set out to explore that process in drama."

The series is currently in development, and we aim to start pre-production in 2022. To see my stories and ideas come to life in this way has been the most beautiful and rewarding experience of this writing project. Seeing that so many other creative people see the value in telling these stories is also very humbling and satisfying. I must once again thank Matt for his support throughout the writing of this book. For the incredible work his have done in making the treatment for Social Media, The Seven Deadly Sins TV show an amazing piece of work.

READ A BOOK

If you have made it this far, thank you. You managed not to be too distracted by your phone or social media channels and read the book. I am grateful for that. When I deleted Instagram and Facebook from my phone I suddenly realised how much extra time I had each day. I decided to use this time to read more. What I found was that I could now read on average a book a week. This was remarkable for me and it illustrated so starkly how much time I have wasted staring into the screen. Social media was a part of my everyday life and job. I was managing social media pages not only for myself and my own business but for major brands and corporations. Some of these pages can generated tens of thousands of likes, reactions and comments each week. You can only imagine how frenzied my notifications feed was. It was exhausting and consuming all aspects of my life. I turned it off. I deleted the apps. I made a struct rule that I would only look at social media pages during work hours and only in the context of doing my job. Not as an everyday user. This is easier to say than it is to do. Its only when you truly try and stop do you realise the power of addiction and the dopamine junkie you have become. My leg would vibrate as if I was getting a notification from my phone. Yet my phone wasn't even in my pocket nor was it even set to vibrate. My body was trying to fool me into picking up my phone and unlocking the screen. My muscles spasming for the sake of my brain demanding another dopamine hit. This feeling was seriously worrying. After consulting Dr Google, everyone's local GP, it soon became apparent this was called phantom vibration syndrome. The cause of phantom vibrations is not yet known. Preliminary research suggests it is related to over-involvement with one's cell phone. My opinion is that further studies will reveal a direct link to notification addiction and a rewiring of the brain through the excessive amounts of screen times spent on social media on our phones.

With this in mind, its time to put down the phone. Turn it off. Start using your time in a different way. Read more books. It was through reading each day that I got inspired and confident enough to write this book. So I wanted to share with you a list of books I found insightful in both my work in brand and marketing strategy as well as in the research for Social Media and the Seven Deadly Sins.

Here is a short list of a few books I found useful in my career.

Advertising & Creative Strategy

- The brand new strategic brand management - Kapferer
- The art of thinking clearly - Rolf Dobelli
- Building a story brand - Donald Miller
- Creativity Inc - Ed Catmul

Behavioural Insights

- Thinking, fast and slow - Daniel Kahneman
- The power of habbit - Charles Duhigg
- Everybody lies - Seth Stephens-Davidowitz
- Inside the nudge unit - David Halpern
- Nudge - Richard H.Thaler, Cass R. Sunstein
- Irrationality - Stuart Suitherland

Technology & Social media

- Facebook the inside story - Steven Levey
- The age of surveillance capitalism - Shoshana Zuboff
- Chaos Monkeys - Antonio Garcia Martinez
- Big data - Vikto Mayer-Schonberger, Kenneth Cukier
- Permanent record - Edward Snowden
- Analysing social networks with Nodexl - Derek L. Hansen, Ben Shneiderman, Marc A. Smith
- No Filter - Sarah Frier

For more book recommendations you can visit my website www.rorywilmer.com

Thank you for reading. Log off and go and enjoy some fresh air.

DO NOT LIKE, SUBSCRIBE OR COMMENT.

15. A POSTSCRIPT

YOU SAY YOU WANT A REVOLUTION

AT THE START of this book, I spoke of Alexei Navalny and the uprising of protests against his detention. A Moscow court on 2 February replaced Navalny's three and a half year suspended sentence with a prison sentence, minus the amount of time he spent under house arrest, meaning he would spend over two and half years in a corrective labour colony where he remains. His health has deteriorated, and his long term prospects look bleak. Returning home to Russia was, it seems, his death sentence.

Protests continue in Belarus; at the time of publishing this book, it was over a year since they began. Since starting this book and mentioning the protests in CHAPTER 3, many deaths and assignations of opposition and pro-democracy figures have been mentioned. President Alexander Lukashenko remains in power, with the full support of Vladimir Vladimirovich Putin.

Social media alone is not enough to dethrone these two hardmen of the post soviet era to bring them down for a more prosperous, democratic and less corrupted future for the people of these godforsaken countries.

Без труда не вытащишь и рыбку из пруда

BLOWING THE WHISTLE

IN BETWEEN WRITING the eBook and preparing for this book's hardback and paperback editions, something monumental happened. During the last weeks of September 2021, The Wall Street Journal published a deep dive investigation titled "The Facebook Files". Based on the evidence submitted by a Facebook employee who turned whistleblower, the WSJ investigation uncovered that Facebook Inc knows exactly the harm its platform is doing to people yet chooses to ignore it so as not to jeopardise its profit margins.

"Facebook Inc. knows, in acute detail, that its platforms are riddled with flaws that cause harm, often in ways only the company fully understands. The central finding of a Wall Street Journal series is based on a review of internal Facebook documents, including research reports, online employee discussions, and drafts of presentations to senior management. Time and again, the documents show, Facebook's researchers have identified the platform's ill effects. Time and again, despite congressional hearings, its pledges and numerous media exposés, the company didn't fix them. The documents offer perhaps the clearest picture thus far of how broadly Facebook's problems are known inside the company, up to the chief executive himself."

You can read the files and full investigation here

https://www.wsj.com/articles/the-facebook-files-11631713039

The revelations were explosive as, for the first time, it started to shine a light deep within Facebook Inc and the suspicion that the company knows very well the harm it is doing to people, yet chooses to ignore and deny it publicly. Much of the report and investigation validates the claims made in this book and coincides perfectly with my messages and my clearing of consciousness and blowing the whistle on social media addiction and how it is harmful and used in a detrimental way to individual health and to broader society. Facebook Inc wheeled out Nick Clegg, the former leader of the Liberal Democrat party in the UK who was once a Deputy Prime Minister in the Liberal/Conservative government led by David Cameroon. After leaving politics, having taken the Liberal Democrat party to one of their worst electoral defeats, Mr Clegg took a £2.7m job as a lobbyist for Facebook under the title of "vice president for global affairs and communications". This basically translates into Mr Clegg becoming the fall guy Facebook wheels out to defend the company's ever-increasing privacy failures and PR disasters [1]. Needless to say, Facebook Inc harness his political connections and reach behind the scenes to hard lobby on behalf of the company.

Within a week or two of the Wall Street Journal's

---

[1] 'Insufficient and very defensive': how Nick Clegg became the fall guy for Facebook's failures https://www.theguardian.com/politics/2021/oct/14/insufficient-very-defensive-how-nick-clegg-became-fall-guy-facebook-failures

Facebook Files investigation, Frances Haugen named herself the whistleblower and went public with her story and testimony. Frances Haugen, 37, who worked as a product manager on the civic integrity team at Facebook, was interviewed by CBS News [2]. This lead to Frances Haugen testifying about Facebook before a US Senate committee on 5 October 2021 [3].

I have total admiration and respect for Frances, who is very brave for speaking out, knowing full well that Facebook Inc will use the full power of their wealth and legal teams to stomp all over her and shut down or dismiss her whistleblowing. Frances revelations led to Nobel Peace Prize-winning journalist Maria Ressa declaring that social media algorithms have introduced "a virus of lies". Maria Ressa compares them to "an atom bomb exploding in our information ecosystem [4]."

While there have been many whistleblowers before Frances, and there will hopefully be many more to come, her moment in time is pivotal for the mass intervention required to shake us all from our social media addictions. It is time now for action, for the truth to be told about how we have become addicted to social media and how our psychographic insights and personal data is used against us in a daily game of persuasion and manipulation in the support of ever-increasing profits for the

2 Frances Haugen: Facebook whistleblower reveals identity https://www.bbc.com/news/technolo-gy-58784615
3 Facebook Whistleblower Frances Haugen testifies before Senate Commerce Committee https://www.youtube.com/watch?v=GOnpVQnv5Cw
4 Facebook is 'biased against facts', says Nobel prize winner https://www.theguardian.com/tech-nology/2021/oct/09/facebook-biased-against-facts-nobel-peace-prize-winner-philippines-ma-ria-ressa-misinformation

surveillance capitalists who now rule our world as we obliviously stare into our phones in search of engagements. "Like" junkies. Emoji zombies.

Time Magazine, during October 2021, published a front cover with the image of Mark Zuckerberg and the dialogue box superimposed over his face with the word DELETE FACEBOOK. In 10 years, TIME magazine has gone from considering Zuckerberg' Person of the Year' to eliminating his social network. We should all take their advice.

DELETE FACEBOOK.

// ENDS

Rory Wilmer

Published by Kindle Direct Publishing

Account ID: ABVGAD55O0NC5

Cover design by www.crystaldinosaur.co.uk

Printed in Great Britain
by Amazon